Martin E. Marty

The Pro & Con Book of Religious America

A Bicentennial Argument

Martin E. Marty

The Pro & Con Book of Religious America

A Bicentennial Argument

PRO

Word Books, Publisher
Waco, Texas

The Pro and Con Book of Religious America

Library of Congress catalog card number: 74–27478

To
John Baumgaertner

A leader, "pro" faith

Contents

Preface

THIS BOOK tries to tell in brief outline what is right—religiously and spiritually—about the two-hundred-year-old United States. The reader who feels it is one-sided need merely flip it over to read the other side since the second half of the book tells what is wrong about the same nation. Each chapter has a counterpart. This format is designed to stimulate creative debate within and among persons during the years surrounding the bicentennial observance—though I hope it will be useful for many years to come since it deals with what may be among the most important issues with which America has to wrestle.

The two halves of the book can each be read in a sitting or two. However, the reader may wish to intersperse chapters from one half with those that are their counterparts in the other half. Or the twelve themes can be taken up by discussion groups, congregations, or classes, through twelve months. The chapters are kept brief for this purpose. They are exactly what they claim to be: arguments. They are not anecdotally crammed. They are not allegories or epic narratives. They are succinct and economical, designed to inspire readers, singly or in groups, to fill in the details out of their own experience, observation, or reading.

Each chapter begins with several paragraphs outlining the spiritual, national, or personal value of the theme. Then readers are invited to look around them, to seek signs or confirmations of that theme and argument in the contemporary world that is in range of their vision, to think about that reality in a special way. Finally, each chapter has several pages on main themes or events from the past. These usually deal with colonial, revolutionary, nineteenth century, or contemporary historical motifs. The proportions of the chapter are shaped so that both those who have interest and competence in history and those that do not (or think they do not) will find themselves addressed. Because the American spirit has been shaped more by biblical faith, Jewish and especially Christian, it has been most frequently assumed or elaborated upon, though some attention has also been devoted to other varieties of religion.

Why such a book? The author has reason to have four worries about readers' responses. They might ask: Is it all a game, arranged for point-scorers in debating societies? If the author sees both sides, is he for a kind of middling and even wishy-washy course between the extremes? Can he really mean what he says in both PRO and CON halves, or are his fingers crossed, is he tongue-in-cheek? Can he be thoughtful; has he thought things through and is his mind clear?

The readers or users will judge, but they are not likely to resent my stating the case. Think of the arrangement as a game, if by this is meant that the experience of struggling with such themes can be creative and pleasurable. But its goal is not for debating points in contests so much as for helping people make up their mind about decisive issues. Almost never does it settle for compromises. Instead, I believe that if people can live with contradiction and paradox, they will learn more from the extremes of national life than from carefully balanced and compromised paragraphs. Third, does he mean it? Yes. I believe that I can back up and richly document the assertions in both halves, and I know that I believe everything I have written about each—and yet have seldom been accused of having a divided mind or being schizoid. American history itself is full of extremes, of paradox, contradiction, and complexity. The ability to live with that history can be health-giving. Finally, I hope that I am thoughtful. The book distills and condenses elements of a career-long concern for American religious history and the spiritual dimensions of today's culture. In such a short book one cannot say everything that should be said about these concerns, but what is said can represent the larger story.

At bicentennial time reflective people can look around them in the present and also backward toward the past in order to move responsibly into the early decades of the nation's third century. This book argues that theme and samples twelve illustrative subthemes.

—MARTIN E. MARTY
Chicago, Illinois

Part I
The American Spirit

1. A Spiritual Society
    versus A Materialistic Society
2. Historical Awareness
    versus Amnesia and Present-Mindedness
3. The Spirit of Community
    versus The Lonely Individualist
4. An International Ethos
    versus Provincialism and Nationalism

-1-

A Spiritual Society

AMERICA is a land of astonishing spiritual vitality. The nation has been impressively, even surprisingly, creative in the things of the soul. This can be said without qualifications, especially to those who have overlooked this feature of national life. Why they have overlooked it might prove to be a productive question. It could be that they have been distracted by their obsession with the United States' parallel productiveness in the material realm. More likely, people have not noticed spiritual achievement because their eyes have been trained to look for other, earlier styles of piety. The definitions may be limiting, the expectations high. Or people may bring ideas and ideologies that would not allow for fertility in this realm. They act as if true depth belongs to the past, to earlier stages of the human race. In those terms, nothing can happen here.

In 1951 the United States Supreme Court, in a sentence that was picked up slightly a decade later in rulings against prayer in public schools, announced that "We are a religious people . . . ." That dictum differs vastly from the often proud and self-righteous statements of presidents at their inaugurals. They like to announce to an insecure people that America is great because she is good, that all is well with her soul. After the people are reassured, they can go about their business again. The Supreme Court's word had a different intention. The justices were not complaining or bragging but were trying to define an aspect of nationhood. If we are a religious people, we can be expected to act one way; if not, we can expect a different course of action.

Some may argue that there is a difference between the opinion that we are spiritual and the fact that we are religious. Religiousness can be skin-deep and full of hypocrisy. For the moment, however, let the two statements be blurred together for purposes of further examination. Criticism can follow after the case for pious America, in the good sense of that term, has been made. The beginning has to do with external measurements. Something has to be going on in a nation where three out of five people list themselves as church members two hundred years after most of their original states removed all legal sanctions for religion. No threat of hell or punishment goes with neglect of worship, and society has few positive goods to pass out to the faithful. Yet after all that time over 60 percent of the people want to be found among the religious, just as over nine out of ten of them are quite clear in telling pollsters that they believe in God.

Membership can be very casual, and can reflect little more than old habits. More significant is the fact that two out of five Americans can be found at worship every weekend. That figure is from ten to twenty times as high as would be found in most European nations, whence the majority of Americans' ancestors came and where many of the critics of religious superficiality still reside.

For a decade or two these church and synagogue goers gave almost one billion dollars per year to religious edifices until they had caught up with the great suburban move or made up for the necessary neglect of church building through two decades of depression and war. They now give support to more than 250 denominations, enough that virtually everyone's needs can be met. If they are not met, people are free to gather to form still other organizations.

These are only clues; they have to do with institutional life. A critic could say that these are all false clues, designed to mislead people and put them on the trail to an America that does not really exist. Before we probe deeper behind the external statistical hints, it is worthwhile to ask why anyone should care how religious or spiritual America may be. Several reasons can be adduced.

First, a nation must define itself somehow. In the case of the United States, made up as it is of fifty states, many peoples, and countless traditions, definition has to go on constantly. People have to tell believable and, they hope, true stories about themselves so that they can have a basis for action.

That tendency leads to the second reason: People define themselves in order to know how to decide about life. If I am in an environment conducive to religion, I must be aware of the situation, lest I fall into hypocrisy and self-deceit. If the setting is hostile, it is important to know what sacrifices might be exacted or expected. To be religious in a monastery brings one set of temptations; to be so in a concentration camp produces different needs.

A third reason for the defining has to do with America among the nations. It is useful for self-understanding when attacks come from others or when they laud a nation's directions, to have a clear picture of reality. One reason why American religiousness is impressive has to do with the surprise that anything spiritual survived at all in its rise. A glance at the human timetable suggests that by 1776 thoughtful people should not have been concerned with the sacred.

Picture, if you can, the world as it looked to the most intelligent people at the time America was born. This is not difficult to do because the people of the Enlightenment Age left many clear writings. They were remarkably consistent. In their views, the New World could perfect what Europe had only begun to face because of the burden of its traditions. In the New World people could be free at last of superstition and dogma. Sacred books of the past gave false mythological accounts of reality. The new people of philosophy and science would be more accurate, more realistic. They could determine how the world had been created, toward what end.

The future might not be wholly nonreligious, but its religion would have a different character. It would be reasonable and reasoned, natural and nonmiraculous. Sacred books would be replaced by catalogs and encyclopedias. It was prehistoric or primitive man who arranged his life around the rhythms of the lives of supposed gods. It was religious man, who was being replaced after thousands of years, who needed supernatural explanations for everything that occurred. In their place would rise a new kind of human who would have dominance over nature and who could take command in history. A *novus ordo seclorum* (see your dollar bill), a new order of ages, was being born in the northern half of the Western Hemisphere.

These European philosophes and their American counterparts (Franklin, Jefferson, Washington, and others) were not all hostile to religion, though they were impatient with its current expression and suspicious of "the priests." They would let some moral example survive from the religious past, but would place it in new contexts. They would turn people's attention from the promise of heaven to the tasks of building the earth. Bad religious forms would wither, though the struggle against them would not at first be easy.

Most historians now agree that such a vision was not outlandish or outrageous. Very few Americans belonged to, attended, or supported religious organizations in the 1770s through the 1790s. The task of creating a new political society drew talents that had gone into the clergy in colonial times. The New World meant the end of old religion. Those who saw matters otherwise were on the defensive.

In spite of the predictions, America turned out to

be very religious. Since the term will appear frequently on these pages, something by way of definition has to be offered. By religion we shall not mean simply what is confined in institutions like churches and synagogues, though we shall never neglect them. Religion has to do with whatever people give final significance to, especially if they tell the story of this significance in the language of myths and symbols, if they gather for rituals and ceremonies to support it, give special explanations of what goes on behind the visible reality, prop it up in social forms, and produce special behavior patterns. On these terms America itself can become the bearer or the object of religious meaning, as can astrology, for example.

With that kind of provisional outline in mind, a nation at bicentennial time can look at its past and see how constant the religious preoccupation has been. The outline of the colonial period remains obvious, even to those who know little about it. If anything, they will tend to magnify and exaggerate the colonial achievements. The explorers from Catholic Europe, in the wake of Columbus, without exception justified their endeavors by reference to what God willed. Their chaplains and missionaries not only interpreted life for them but extended a sense of the Christian's concept of God into a new hemisphere.

Virginians are often treated as casual worshipers, but they did bring their pastors, too, and they made provisions wherever they settled along the rivers to make the parish church a center of their life. They in-

cluded missions to Indians in their charters, and per-
petuated a form of church existence that still attracted
the loyalty if not the passion of the nation's elite founding fathers. In the Middle Colonies most people came
for religious reasons: Quakers, Mennonites, Dunkers,
Lutherans, Anabaptists—persecuted in Europe—
came to America out of conviction, and took pains to
assure the centrality of Christianity in their preoccupations. No one need deny the economic interests they
had, but they also underwent sacrifices for the sake of
their heritages and the future.

New England's story is most familiar. From the
diaries and records of the Bradfords and Winthrops,
the Winslows and Mathers, later generations can see
that these fathers and mothers saw their actions as an
extension of a great biblical drama. Whatever they
did was foreseen or paralleled in the Book of Exodus
or other writings that told of a people rescued from
plight and sent on an errand into the wilderness. In a
sense they knew the outcome of history; they were living out a script they had seen in advance. The smallest
details of daily life were prefigured or interpreted by
Scriptures. The common people knew their place and
found meaning in their toil, just as their rulers took
seriously the sense that God had given them a man-
date. The images of New England that have survived
into later times are largely religious: of Thanksgiving
days, great awakenings, meetinghouses, religious
laws, the Sabbath, etc. If later generations have sometimes scored the Puritans for their severities, they

have also come to appreciate the majesty of their thought-patterns and the sincerity with which they worked out religious grasps of reality.

The American representatives of the Enlightenment, to whom we made reference earlier, should also not be seen to be nonreligious so much as they were advocates of a new tolerant religious spirit. They were devising a new religion of the human spirit, full of progress and optimism. Some sort of deity survived (in a system often called deistic). If this was not the warm or judging personal God of the Bible, there was still a sense of order, moral purpose, historic meaning in the witness. Later America, often unaware of the extent of deviation these expressed over against the historic faith, had images of reverent and God-fearing founding fathers and fashioners of this two-century old republic.

The turn of the pages in history books to the nineteenth century opens a whole and surprising second chapter. The dreams of the philosophes were denied. People could not all be content with simple rational explanations of their world of wonders. In the great outpouring of revivals they frankly embraced biblical supernaturalism. They wanted and found religions of experience, often rich in emotion and productive of the works of love. A period of frantic evangelizing followed, as America became "churched." New denominations, the Baptist, Methodist, and Disciples of Christ paralleled and then outstripped the colonial big three, the Presbyterian, Episcopal, and Congregational churches. Immigrants from the continent found new prosperity in Lutheran, Reformed, and Roman Catholic churches. In that environment people who tried the existing faiths also picked up new accents, and the Latter Day Saints or Seventh Day Adventists joined their counterparts and led to the formation of numbers of new faiths.

What about those for whom the churches were not satisfying? It would be hard to look back now, after the controversies have died, and accuse them of being less serious about things of the spirit. For example, the main literary tradition found expression in the writings of transcendentalists: the Emersons, Parkers, Alcotts, and Thoreaus. Most of them rejected historic Christianity because they felt it was not religious enough. It recalled dead kings and remembered sepulchres, and offered encrusted dogmas and narrow patterns of piety and works. The transcendentalists and subsequent writers would replace the old piety with a new one, in "the party of hope," full of freedom and flux. The poets have taken up their themes and offered alternatives throughout subsequent history.

The twentieth century has been no less productive of ritual or religious explanation. After the World's Parliament of Religions in Chicago in 1893, or as a result of some Eastern and African representatives and visitors, nonwestern faiths made their way. In the 1960s and 1970s almost every religion ever known to man, including astrology, occult faiths, and metaphysical cults, found significant followings.

Nor was the landscape barren of spiritually complex and innovative people: Thomas Merton, E. Stanley Jones, Dorothy Day, Harry Emerson Fosdick, Daniel Berrigan, Alan Watts, Dag Hammarskjøld, countless mystics, holy men and women, gurus, shamans, and cult leaders, priests, ministers, rabbis, lay leaders, saints, and scholars kept alive the variety of spiritual expressions. Monasteries flourished and languished; then communes took their place; parishes prospered and suffered; house churches took up some of the slack. There were few signs of slowing down. Father Andrew Greeley early in the 1970s decided that people were as religious as they had ever been, and that America offered as wide a range of options as any place.

The question of quality is another matter. The tawdry and exploitative was there alongside the rarer more profound versions. What has to be established here is that despite claims about its materialism, America has been a hospice for men and women in their spiritual quests and has given encouragement to their expressions. They seek meaning and belonging, and the American environment offers them a place for the questions and some answers. Their world is not all external and self-explanatory. They seek the things of spirit and soul.

-2-

Historical Awareness

DURING THE half-dozen years in which the American Bicentennial observance was being planned, there were many criticisms about the character of the event. Some of the proposals were purely commercial; people naturally wanted to make money off a nation's celebration of its survival after two centuries. Other analysts felt that no one knew what was being celebrated; after the war in Vietnam, the scandals symbolized by the word Watergate, and in the midst of disputes over the energy crisis and the economy, all the brouhaha and to-do about events of 1776 looked like escapism and evasion. Why should people take refuge in a remote past, and why should they congratulate themselves for being mere heirs of traditions they were doing so little to keep alive and healthy?

America's spiritual forces also were swept up in bicentennial debates, and the churches and synagogues undertook many steps to share in the observance. Many of the ceremonies may amount to little more than flag-waving, to a confusion of God and country, or to antiquarianism in the face of a world that today displays so much hunger, despair, and physical or psychic need. This is not the moment to engage in extensive scrutinies of either the secular or religious bicentennial events; instead, it can be used to lift out an often-neglected element in the American past.

In the face of well-founded and more than half-true charges that Americans are too obsessed with present and future to know who they are, whence they have come, and what they should hope for, the bicentennial fuss and feathers can also demonstrate that one side of the American character is indeed responsive to the past. This does not mean that citizens are all turning into professional historians; there may be already too many of these. (Ask the new Ph.D who is trying to get a job in history or to have his book manuscript lifted out of waiting-line obscurity and published.) It does mean that professionals are joined by millions of amateurs in showing, sometimes appropriately and sometimes pathetically, a curiosity about and a love for the story of the past and of their past. In all this there is at least some dim sense that history matters for today and tomorrow.

Such a suggestion runs against the American grain. In folklore, Henry Ford was a hero for having said that "history is bunk!" Millions of Americans who endured boring and pointless history classes in high school are not usually seen as lovers of history. In a world of scientific and technological reasoning or in a world shaped by the immediate impressions that mass media can communicate, we are constantly being told that we have forgotten historical means of arguing and reasoning, that we cannot and do not want to derive meaning from the story of the past or a sense of tradition. Even many professional historians admit that they have lost belief in the potential power of their stories and pursue them despite the fact that history offers neither power nor meaning nor hope.

Why does the study of history, the past, and the tradition become an important subject in such a culture? The best answer, both for the individual and for society, is that history can make at least a modest contribution to our identity and thus to our well-being. It is a part of our self-understanding, because it locates us in a landscape whose terms and images have been inherited. They influence whether or not we understand their sources in the past; when we understand the past, we can take a better part in shaping the future. As nineteenth-century German social thinkers and historians like Ernst Troeltsch and Adolf Harnack were wont to say, we study history to overcome history, to intervene in history, to know when and where and how to act in history.

These questions are especially urgent in America's major religious contexts, among Jews, Christians, and others who draw on the Bible and other historic documents for the resources of faith. Biblical religion is an historic faith, which asks people to find the eternal and timeless questions addressed in the drama of the temporal (Nikolai Berdyaev). For Christians this drama does not occur as a transaction out in the clouds and with angels. The biblical Letter to the Hebrews reasons by pointing to Jesus Christ that God acts in history, among his people and through his prophets. Most decisively, he spoke through his Son, who became a man in the midst of human history. "We are to history as fish are to water," said the American theologian H. Richard Niebuhr. "We cannot escape history," was Abraham Lincoln's sense of how the past presents problems and decisions or opportunities for people.

We are not conscious of being involved in history at all times; it is possible to be too preoccupied with the past to be spiritually free for the present. We are historians when we "stop to think." We do so in crisis or uncertainty. Like individual persons, a society through history thus has a memory that interrupts routine and thoughtless life. Abraham Lincoln also said that if we could first know where we are and whither we are tending we might know what to do and how to do it—and this knowing can come only from an understanding of the past.

People have found that becoming aware of the past gives them identity and a participation in the divine–human drama. There are other benefits that can be recognized in the seasons when the whole nation recalls its own founding two centuries ago. History can also be liberating. Citizens learn that many past resolutions no longer apply, and have to be rejected. They may recognize that the nation has survived many crises and transformations, and from that may take courage to outlast current crises of change. In Christian circles something similar is operative.

Let me give one illustration about the liberating feature of history. In today's America people are aware that many religious forms are in cultural trouble. Among these are the denomination, the Sunday school, the network of voluntary associations and societies that accompany religious organizations, the modern form of sending and supporting missionaries and then of interpreting their work, and the competitive local church or parish pattern. Unquestionably, when these are in trouble religion is in trouble, for the spiritual energies of most Americans are focused through these or something like them. But when one becomes aware of history, it is obvious that these five forms or patterns, were invented or developed within a few decades of the magic year 1776.

For almost eighteen centuries Christians did not have denominations. These could only be born in the era of religious freedom that came with the American Revolution. Until then they knew only established churches *versus* dissenting churches, and not churches that were legally on a par with each other. Sunday schools were born in England and developed in America after 1786 to meet the new needs and opportunities that went with the Industrial Revolution, political democracy, and evangelical revival. The voluntary societies for reform and mission became complex and sophisticated in the first four decades of the nineteenth century. The missionary agencies, elites, and ethos developed in several continental countries but especially in England and America after the 1790s and in the early years of the new century. Old geographical parish patterns that dated from the fourth century were changed to competitive and overlapping parish boundaries when denominations were born, revivals occurred, and a frontier beckoned.

Is it not liberating to learn, then, that the forms that are in trouble today were not present in recognizable form for eighteen-nineteenths of Christian history? Could it be that in the third century of national life believers are called to allow or urge transforming of these patterns and developing new ones—out of the materials gained, to be sure, from the past?

Americans recognize these spiritual possibilities in the sense of history and tradition and show signs of awakening to the importance of the subject. It is not likely that they will be overwhelmed by those who suffer from the "dead hand of tradition," who make hobbies of history and are mere antiquarians, or who use history only for debunking purposes. American society offers enough checks against their victory simply because most pressures come from a sense of openness and a passion for the new. But in the conflict between these pressures, a new appreciation for the values of history and tradition is being developed.

At bicentennial time we are aware of our Williamsburgs and Sturbridge Villages, our Alamos and Mount Vernons, our reconstructions and relics of a living past. We see people making pilgrimages to such shrines. In the religious world there are evidences of a growing of concern with the story of the faiths of America during these two centuries of national life or the two centuries of colonial precedent. The arguments over that history will enliven national life and provide the churches with new bases for reform and renewal. But the current stirrings and activities are themselves rooted in attitudes that were long present, if not always so visible as they are today.

In colonial America it is true that the immigrants often turned their back on the Europe that had persecuted or ejected them or deprived them of liberty. It is also true that they often were intoxicated with the future that the new environment offered. But they did not lose the sense of history, and in selective ways kept it alive. Thus the fathers of many colonies joined the New Englanders who at least reached to the Bible as a paradigm or model for their history. They read of the exodus and exile of God's ancient people and saw meaning in their story as they reenacted these themes in a new landscape. They were conscious not only of biblical history, but often had a true regard for Greek and Roman antiquity.

The historian Henry Steele Commager points to their historic sense in his essay *The Search for a Usable Past*. He showed how they could adopt all of the past, all of Europe, and could acquire instant ancestors as their own ancestors could not in their own segregated valleys and villages in Europe. They immediately had a sense of the importance of their own past; they became ancestors very quickly! By 1776 many of them talked about "the olden days" of the first Great Awakening or spiritual revival—even though it had occurred only two-score years earlier. They saw in the events of their revolution a new chapter in a "kind providence's" dealing with them as he had dealt with his people in the past.

While the political leaders and framers of the nation's founding documents were formally given over to some anti-historical Enlightenment attitudes and devoted themselves to study of nature and science, they also could not shrug off history. Some of them studied the Bible for precedent; more of them derived spiritual themes that were useful in politics from the philosophy and law of classic Greek and Roman times.

The historical sense became more complicated in the nineteenth century. At first the "historians against history" rejected the complexities of European history and gave the impression of having no regard for the creative character of the past. But they did find it valid to tell the story of the American people on grand and epic scales. George Bancroft, Francis Parkman, and other pioneers became more or less religious prophets who pondered the meaning of the American spirit and experience. The spiritual side of the political tradition came to a climax in Abraham Lincoln, a leader who had a true sense of the weight and limits imposed by the past and the liberation that could come to people who wrestled with that past.

The American churches meanwhile often gave the appearance of trying to do what Lincoln said could not be done. They tried to escape history. Some of them by advocating a "primitive gospel" often acted as if God could unfold his will only during the decade or two when Jesus Christ and his apostles were engaged in the acts recorded in the New Testament. Others of them tried to escape history by taking refuge in doctrines and dogmas codified in catechisms and textbooks, forgetting that these teachings were also shaped by the communities of the past and the languages and ideas that had lived in the Christian or other religious communities of the past.

Primitivism and dogmatism do not make up the whole past, however. In the course of the century America's religionists began to recognize the values that came from the past. Sometimes this recognition took romantic form. Thus many of them tried to make the Middle Ages their own, at least in stone. In the middle of the century there was an amazing revival of Gothic architecture, a medieval form. The people who used it—and some of them made good creations out of these patterns—may often have had a mere antique-shop sense and may have retarded the development of new appropriate architectural forms. But they at the same time responded to something deep in the human spirit and the religious sense. They felt that by reaching back they could anchor themselves in the midst of new storms. They could spiritually associate with people who had gone before. The Middle Ages began to be rediscovered by the very Protestants who had repudiated them. Some of the continental immigrants brought with them senses of history that led others to reexplore the continental Reformation of Calvin and Luther or the long centuries of Roman Catholic witness. Even the primitives and the dogmatists made some contributions, however compromising these might be. They did suggest that at least some moment or moments in the past could speak to the present.

By the time of the nation's centennial, 1876, the days of simple repudiation of the past seemed to be passing. Americans relished their history. While the exhibits at their expositions may have been preoccupied with science and invention, the event as a whole inspired reflection on the past. Meanwhile the modern university was developing; it housed history departments that took long looks at the religious past and theological schools that tried to help people look at problems that a sense of history brought. These problems included a critical awareness about flaws in the past and the sense that "everything is relative," a sense that often causes doubts when it first hits believers. These modern thinkers often went about their task in strange ways, but their intention was to help people continue to believe and to express their faith in ways that showed both an awareness of the past with its complexity and a sense of freedom from whatever in the past made people slaves of tradition, habit, and custom. Their task remains half-finished today.

- 3 -

The Spirit of Community

RELIGIOUS AMERICA has been and is conducive to the building of human community. To say so in bright, upbeat tones suggests that community is a spiritual good. Those who have experienced its depths would be the first to agree. Those who have experienced little but who claim to be moved by the Bible, know that these sacred Scriptures speak of human life as essentially social. While the modern world and even modern religion occasionally fall into the trap of advertising religion as being an individual matter, born of "the right of private judgment," historic Judaism and Christianity—like most other religions—have been intensely communitarian.

In the Hebrew Scriptures, man is what he is first of all as part of the *Qehal Yahweh,* the gathered congregation of Yahweh. People emerge from their tribe, clan, and family which provide them with support and encouragement, the security out of which person-

The Spirit of Community

ality develops. Often the Old Testament will give only a paragraph or two about a personality and we feel we know his character better than we do that of someone who is covered today in a two-volume biography. Why? Because his personhood emerged against a background of securities and expectations. He was established and had an identity.

In the New Testament these accents are enhanced and given universal scope. The church is "the body of Christ," a single extension having many members. Most of the metaphors of Christian relations to God are plural, social, and dynamic: they have to do with the people of God, with a pilgrim band, a flock, with branches of a vine. Persons matter, but they are born, they grow up, they live and suffer, worship and rise with "the new people of God." Paul's concern is not simply with how to rescue a person out of the world but rather with how Jews and gentiles, in both of whom the spirit of Christ has become active, can live together in one church. In the First Letter to the Corinthians he shows how the sin of one stains a whole congregation.

Most students of personality carry these motifs over into modern life and show how instability and alienation result when people have to make their own way apart from community. The modern world has plenty of room and need for misfits, individualists, mavericks, angular or square pegs for society's round holes. They picture community turning authoritarian and totalitarian, society being subtly oppressive or repressive. But rarely if ever do they picture true health or wholeness growing except in the context of community. One of the measures of religious America, then, has to be the question of how people find and express life together.

A view around the 360-degree circle of vision shows that American religiousness offers many kinds of community. Few people have been as free as are contemporary Americans to feel themselves a part of "the family of man." Many in India's 400,000 villages will pass their life without ever seeing anyone from another village; few of them will ever have a clear image of other ways of life brought by radio, television, or the press. But in the developed nations the media, travel, and mass education bring these images into the sphere of people's daily consciousness. They have practical dealings with people throughout the global village and in many corners of spaceship earth.

Religion plays a part in this developed consciousness. In American colleges, for example, the offerings in religion are particularly rich. A Methodist coed studies with a Jewish young man in a class taught by a Catholic and having to do with Buddhist or Hindu texts. Their parents subscribe to a series of books or watch television programs depicting the faiths of other people. These studies go on with less sense of distance and hostility than ever before. In a way the new awareness builds a sense of world community. Few minimize the profound differences between faiths; but they try to appropriate something of life in other social spheres.

In the past these religions might have been viewed

with more suspicion by Christians during the great years of their missionary ventures. People are more supportive of missions if they feel that they are helping people replace something bad rather than build on something good. So the old missionaries came back with horrendous stories of idolatry and superstition. Yet even then they were preparing people to comprehend a larger human community. The fact that Jesus Christ died for *all people* had long been asserted in Christianity. Now these people were coming into Christians' ken. Americans were as busy as anyone in sending missionaries and telling their stories.

Religious America therefore need not blush in comparison with secular America, so far as consciousness of the family of man is concerned. In a typical community a program designed to make the workings of the UN or UNESCO known would attract only a tiny audience. But in church after church many nights of the week or many a Sunday, world needs keep on being beamed at people. While statistically much smaller, the Jewish people—especially because of their ties to Israel—have even more sense of "peoplehood" and the need for world community. Correspondence between mission fields or younger churches and their sponsors, prayer chains, and the like, increase awareness between religious people here as elsewhere.

The mass media are at home in America, and they breed certain kinds of community. Admittedly, these are somewhat superficial. The media tend to have to do with the play, not the work hours of life. They touch our notions, opinions, attitudes, and fad-life more than our central belief systems. Yet people are alert to the doings of Pope Paul and Billy Graham; they support "The Lutheran Hour" or "The Catholic Hour." In such programs they see their local symbols tried out on a world-wide audience and find a kind of community developing.

One might say that American Christians have an opportunity to be catholic in both their universal sense and because they can see how religion touches all of life. They derive from European, African, and now, lately, Asian religious movements and are aware of their ties. Despite all that has been said, however, the family of man and the concept of world-wide community may be too broad to be supportive, so the social realm has to be sought closer to home, as well. Religion has built and continues to build national community.

The observer looks first at the nation itself. Intense debates rage about the existence and value of what some professors call "civil religion." In such a faith people use the nation itself as a kind of bearer or revealer of religious significances. The critics say that such a faith is idolatrous, given to justifying whatever the nation does. The advocates, however, point to someone like Abraham Lincoln to show that one can deal positively with the nation and the social order and still see it under divine judgment and in need of divine mercy. People can be loyal and patriotic without making a religion of their loyalty, but it is almost inevitable that they combine national and religious symbols. In America the impulse has been especially strong, because no religious creed held by churches includes enough of them.

Similarly there are some positive features to the ways in which huge subcommunities, Jewish, Catholic, and Protestant, serve to support community. Even the nation seems too large to grasp as a means of offering identity. For that reason, people reach out through large but better defined groupings.

Jews may be denominationalized into Orthodox, Conservative, Liberal, Reform, and Reconstructionist factions, but being a Jew offers its own part in shaping identities. Roman Catholics have been internally divided on ethnic lines, their religious orders have competed, and their dioceses gone their own ways. Still, being Catholic gives them a handle on a larger community. Protestants, because of their division, perhaps have the least sense of commonality, but their enemies or those who stand outside their churches purport to see characteristic Protestant modes that cut across huge sectors of evangelical faiths.

Denominations, parishes, and smaller cells serve even more particularly. Denominations do not exactly parallel the outline of creeds. One knows little about what a person believes if he is told that someone is Methodist, Baptist, or a member of the United Church of Christ. He has to know where the church is located, where the minister studied, what income group is represented, what the politics of the majority of members are, if there is to be any comprehension of what the people are about. Or so it seems to the outsider. Despite this, denominationalism does not go away; it almost seems to be on the increase. Somehow the denomination must satisfy certain needs of people and provide them a measure of community.

When one ranges in on the local congregation the communal aspects are richer and more visible. While not all local churches give people a clear sense of world, national, or even denominational community, they can be very supportive of feltneeds. There may be many huge and impersonal congregations made up of marginal people in a passing parade. But millions of Americans know that in a parish there is a defining support group that ministers to many needs.

Take the example of an older woman whose husband has a terminal illness. If she is a member of a vital parish, she probably does not have to turn to many professional services for chauffeuring, blood transfusions, meeting certain obligations, or finding counsel. She will be immediately surrounded by people who have come to know, care, and feel responsibility for her. Where people do nothing more than make a spiritual pit stop in a Sunday pew, community has little chance to grow, though even there common symbols invoke common themes for shared hopes. But where the church reaches into other elements of life, community does grow. For all its faults, the local church most often "works" at this level, and is the best example of a social orbit in a religious world that is usually seen to be characterized by lonely individuals.

Where parishes do not work, people let cells or interest groups get generated. In our time, house churches, underground churches, para-parishes, or various expressions of the human potential movement have supplied these alternatives. They have their antecedents all the way back to early Methodism.

All these accents have a history. In the colonial period, however, they may be faulted for cutting other people out of their value systems. In the long thin strips of civilization along the rivers of Virginia, Anglicans gathered Sundays for long days of worship and socializing at the parish churches. In the villages and countrysides of Pennsylvania, New Jersey, and New York, churches of small Reformed or Lutheran, Anabaptist or Quaker groups were the magnet and focus of warm supportive community. In New England, despite what later generations sometimes saw to be a contribution to rugged individualism, community was the main goal of church life so far as the needs of this world are concerned.

Community was conceived organically; that is, all the parts were in dynamic relation to each other. The Bible served as a code that outlined it and the elders administered it. No one failed to find his part in it. The concept of the covenant was central. The covenant reached out to all but had to be "owned" by those who would take responsible parts after having a certified religious experience. The sin of one brought travail on all; the conversion of one benefited the fate of all. The social relations and economic conditions or order were planned. The result could be stifling, and much fault can be found in it. But whatever shortcomings

the system had, it was productive of colorful and creative persons who do not seem to have been stifled so
much as they were strengthened by the social character of their faith.

The later history shows a reinforcement of the demand for community against ever greater odds. The
partly settled ways of colonists were replaced by itiner-
ants, travelers, merchants, sailors, visitors, evangelists. The westward trek uprooted people. But instead
of despairing, people expressed desire to make community portable. If they could not have religion in a
settled town, they could come together at a camp meeting. Those who were converted there were initiated
into the larger frontier society and found a place not
only in the church but in the accepted social world.

The cities represented greater difficulties. Churches
could no longer occupy the spatial center of the ever-
changing city as they had once done in the village.
Commerce competed with the churches' claims. New
immigrants arrived. More churches of different denominations struggled for existence. But if a single
church could no longer interpret and give life for all
the inhabitants, individual congregations helped people overcome some of the loneliness and alienation
produced by city life.

If there is any realm in which revision of opinion
still has to occur, it is in that of the frontier. The
American myth brags about the ruggedness and individualism on the frontier. Ruggedness there was;
characters there were. But most pioneers did not regard loneliness as an asset. Instead they usually did

what they could to find life in community. For the majority, the church offered on a more durable and deeper scale what tavern, club, school, or store could not. The appeal of early Methodism and the Baptist churches lay in the immediate sense of community left behind by the circuit rider or traveling evangelist. And on the urban frontier the priest did the same for Catholics; people who had been less religious in traditional European Catholicism found that it paid to work at the faith and be supportive in America. They found themselves by building community.

The story continues against the intensified difficulties of mobile suburban or ghetto America. People have not shown the end of their search for belonging. Not all of them know the means for finding it. Some take refuge in huge high-rise apartments where privacy and anonymity are guarded from pushy and overly gregarious religious forces. But in those places where community is lost, people experience depression and despair as often as they know freedom. America offers nonreligious styles of community, but where there is religion, there is also community among the attractions.

-4-

An International Ethos

THROUGHOUT HISTORY, religions have tended to be tied down to specific localities. Their myths, symbols, and dogmas tend to explain tribal customs. Or they are used to hint at the meaning of natural events that occur on a particular landscape; they explain why a river flows or why water falls where it does. They designate a hill or mountain as sacred, or a valley as a place where a sacred drama will occur. Locality also plays its part in the religions of the world whenever these suggest that people's responsibilities are to be carried out not in some remote cloudland but where they live their daily lives.

Tying down a faith to a location can have both good and bad consequences. It can lead people to appreciate their environment and take their daily life seriously. On the other hand, it can lead to an idolizing of place. The gods are nothing more than tribal deities; when properly appeased they justify anything a particular group of people want to do against others. They prevent people from becoming curious about or taking a positive interest in the doings of others. Religions based on such ideas of deity stand behind many holy wars.

Biblical religion, the cluster of views about reality that has largely informed America's spiritual life, shows both these sides. The Hebrew Scriptures are built around the vision of a promised land; the grand themes of both an exodus and an exile show how the people of Yahweh were to love and were in love with particular soil. But the prophets also began to instruct the people about the dangers of being too provincial in their concept of God.

The New Testament and early Christianity are also born of Jesus' regard for a people in a place, but not only some remembered words of Jesus in the Gospels but especially the writings of Paul picture a faith that embraces the whole world and has meaning for all people everywhere. From that time on a universal vision gave life and breath to much Christian language. While in those earlier days the references dealt more with peoples than with nations, in the modern world the question of nationalism and internationalism, provincialism versus ecumenism or catholicity colors religious life.

In the Christian vision, Jesus Christ's redemptive story can no longer be seen as having to do with only one nation and one people. And since people in all nations can be called by his name, they are then to be concerned with each other. The benefits of brotherhood and neighborliness now reach far beyond tribe and clan or nation. People who love these more remote brothers and sisters live out motifs of Christian empathy and sympathy.

From many points of view, American religion in general, and Christianity in particular, have stood tests of universality. The faith of Americans has tended to be outgoing, one that shows considerable awareness of and concern for others than Americans. Even when the nation had a Monroe Doctrine to exclude many kinds of outside influence, the religious forces broke its bounds in a spiritual sense.

Today the evidences of this spirit appear on all hands, most notably in the ongoing missionary ties of American believers. Scores of millions of Americans are Roman Catholics, tempted as are their fellow citizens to look only to things American. Yet they overcome that temptation whenever they are alert to what it means to be "catholic," to belong to a family of apostolic churches that is represented almost everywhere. While non-Catholics often criticize their attachment to Rome, it may also be said that Rome symbolizes the center of a network that makes Catholic contact with people all over the world possible. In countless parishes offerings are taken for leper colonies in Africa or hospitals in the Orient. It might be said that the United Nations or UNESCO can sponsor similar activities, and these agencies often do. But the ties are often impersonal, temporary, and organized through bureaucracies that interrupt the people-to-people sense that Catholicism has offered.

While most Protestants do not acknowledge a "center" somewhere else as the base from which a worldwide network of service or for interpreting meaning emerges, they are often no less catholic than are Roman Catholics. As a result of nineteenth century British imperialism and missionary efforts, English-speaking people went into all the world. As a consequence, the Anglican Communion of which American Episcopalians are a part, is as catholic as the Roman communion. For two and a half centuries European and, later, American Lutherans went into all the world, so people in this lineage in the United States feel themselves very much a part of a universal confessing group. This is even more true of those churches that were represented most strongly in nineteenth century America and from there went out to the world: the Baptist, Congregational, Methodist, Presbyterian and other groups. Americans are not alone in the Christian world or the world at large.

The ties have been strengthened in many ways. Sunday school literature and countless sermons have been illustrated for a century and a half with reports from missionaries. While the nonchurched American child might learn geography or world affairs, the church-going one has the advantage of having remote places personalized, filled with people they know and about whom they are to care. The returning or visiting missionary has often been satirized as having offered a biased view of the overseas world for local markets. But there were exceptions, and even the biased information at least developed in American Christians a sense of involvement with others. If in the late twentieth century many of the churches have grown tired and uncertain about missions and may even have withdrawn to some extent, the deposit of past years lives on in the memories and lives of church people.

The twentieth century international spirit lives on in many if not in all religious groups. They know better than some of their critics do that not every contact Americans make with people elsewhere are overtly imperialistic or exploitative. For example, the whole concept of Afro-Americanism is an expression of a bond between struggling black people in America and their ancestral world with its ongoing quest for liberation. "Captive nations" in Europe, countries that have been taken over into the Soviet orbit, usually by force, have their Christian spokesmen in America. These spokesmen, sometimes militantly but more often through responsible argument, try to bring millions of eastern Europeans' fates to the attention of their fellow citizens.

American religion, both biblical and of other types, has often contributed to internationalist visions. United World Federalists and scores of other organized groups advocating internationalism have won support particularly from the more liberal American religious groups. One can almost see an interplay here; where people in the United States are not necessarily obsessed with new missionary activities, they tend to stress international brotherhood. Where they are suspicious of the language of brotherhood, federalism, or synthesis, they remain missionary. However different the ideas of both tendencies are, they both keep alive an internationalist sense. In the lives of many people the two motifs coexist.

For a variety of reasons that are not always born of religion, Americans have been especially well poised to have an internationalist sense, one that leads them to counter any tendencies they might have had to make their God into a tribal and local deity. Because they have been technologically advanced travelers and communicators, they have been able to be uncommonly aware of the faiths of other people. It is hard for a Tibetan to have a concept of other people beyond his mountain ranges. Many islanders have only the vaguest ideas of what goes on across the waters. Even less affluent and certainly the less developed nations offer fewer opportunities for a catholic view of humanity. But America can afford and does stimulate travel. It sends and receives students to and from other places. Its very sophisticated television, radio, films, and newspapers help people see the world as others see it. Many resist what they see, or interpret it through provincial glasses. Americans may not have a fully developed sense of stewardship in the world, but by accident of history or design of her people, the United States probably exceeds most nations in its ability to develop a sense of spaceship earth, the global village, or the family of man.

Most important for a theological analysis, it is possible in America to transcend nationalist ideology. Some years ago a friend was commissioned to travel

had been to many ecumenical gatherings where
American nationalism was criticized from abroad.
Certainly the church people from developing nations
and younger churches had lessons to teach us about
transcending, going above and beyond and around national idolatry! He never wrote the book; he found
that these people were gifted at discerning American
religions' ties to the environment. They were at least
as bound up with their own national destiny and identity as his fellow citizens of the United States ever
were.

Thanks to theologians like Reinhold Niebuhr
Americans learned that they could be loyal citizens
and yet know that God sits in judgment on the nations
and *this* nation. "He that sitteth in the heavens shall
laugh." Here advocates of a civil religion, one that
would make the nation a kind of source and center of
many spiritual values, have to take pains to show that
the tie between nation and God is not exclusive and
that the Almighty cannot be called down to justify all
our purposes. In the United States a large church
body can formally confess that this nation may have
to take risks for peace even at the expense of national
security.

All these states of mind and situations emerge out
of a long history of internationalism in American religion. It is true that from the sixteenth to the nineteenth centuries the Orient was hardly known and
Africa was little more than a breeding ground for the

51

people that Americans would reduce to slavery. During that earlier period Europe at least served as a connecting point to a larger world.

At first Europe meant the Mediterranean sphere. The people who first came to these shores, particularly to the southeastern and southwestern part of the United States left a stamp of Spanish and sometimes Portuguese cultures (as a spillover from Central and especially South American cultural ties). In the Catholic phase of colonization, French Europe had an impact on Canada and much of the northeast, the upper midwest, and the Mississippi Valley. But from the seventeenth into the nineteenth century the British Isles and northwest (Protestant) Europe kept American religion attentive to international concerns.

A kind of North Atlantic culture developed in those years. There was an actual transfer of people. The immigrants brought with them the tongues, customs, churches, and faiths of many different groups east of the Atlantic. People kept coming, letters were transmitted, curiosity about the old country and the new land informed the religious groups. Often there would be spiritual movements that had counterparts or representatives on both sides of the Atlantic: Puritanism in Old England and New England; Pietism in continental and middle-colonial Lutheranism; Anabaptism in the Low Countries and the high hills of Pennsylvania; Wesleyanism and Methodism in London and in Georgia; Jansenism among French or Irish and American Roman Catholics. These movements led people on both sides of the Atlantic to look for brotherhood and support among people who saw religion as they did.

The American Enlightenment, an event that has to be celebrated in the years of bicentennial observance, was a thoroughly international and ecumenical affair. The founding fathers of the nation often worked with philosophies and social systems that derived from England and the continent. Some of them devoted much attention, for example, to the political thought of John Locke, an English philosopher. They watched with interest the scientific development of continental philosophes and encyclopedists. The religious ideas that they thought would replace the more conservative American Christian ideas of biblical revelation and miracle were recognized as coming in part from British Deism. People like Benjamin Franklin and Thomas Jefferson were both in person and by correspondence commuters between nations.

While the American revolution may have been of a more conservative character than the French, the fact that new ideas of liberty, equality, and fraternity were being contended for on both sides of the Atlantic promoted spiritual ties—though these ties were to suffer when Americans saw the French and later European revolutions turning more radical. The later Industrial Revolution produced similar problems and solutions on both sides of the water.

From the time of the Monroe Doctrine through World War I, America often retreated into national isolation. But its church people remained somewhat internationally conscious. They were concerned about reports of revivals in European nations. They linked with Europeans in an "errand of mercy" that would reform the world and serve the suffering in it. Movements like those that led to the abolition of slavery were supported by certain kinds of evangelicals on both sides of the Atlantic, even if England abolished slavery a third of a century before America did, and even if the story of American abolition found evangelicals eventually sorely divided.

In the nineteenth century the missionary movement, to which we have already made reference, found Americans busy in all parts of the world. What came to be called the ecumenical movement in our time was foreshadowed in an Evangelical Alliance and in countless less well-known connections between American believers and their European counterparts. There was some, though perhaps not enough, theological interaction transoceanically. Whenever there appeared to be a lessening of ties, new waves of people—in the 1840s from Catholic and after the 1880s from Eastern European Orthodox and Jewish spheres—kept America from lapsing into total provincialism. It was not easy for them to make of their God only a tribal deity who cared only about one place.

Part II
The American People

-5-

Religiously Tolerant Tribes

DESPITE GREAT odds and magnificent opportunities for mischief, America can show a history of religious amity among divided peoples. People who disagree about religious ultimates have characteristically reached for the support of the sword to settle their arguments. If someone feels that he or she has a perfect arrangement with God, a pipeline of answers to life's final questions, there is often a temptation to go a step further and suggest that all others have to step aside. They have no room in the divine plan.

Where the battles are not waged over theological argument, they tend to develop because religions generate styles of living that lead to conflict. Thus in northern Ireland the Protestant is seen as the late intruder who took advantage of the economic situation to gain mastery. The Roman Catholic uses his or her church as a center for definition of a life that seeks redress of old grievances. Economic matters may be prime, but religious symbols and organizations serve to intensify existing battles.

So it is with most areas of the world where wars have religious dimensions. In Vietnam one kind of Buddhist teamed with Roman Catholic refugees from the north to fight a prolonged war over against other kinds of Buddhists, Marxists, and religious nationalists.

In India and Pakistan Hindus and Muslims fight battles that reach back to religious differences of centuries' long standing. African tribesmen, as in Nigeria, wage warfare that is not unmarked by different tribal religious symbols. On these terms, one would expect holy wars to be waged in America.

The variety of options are there. Every phone book, every religious yearbook or encyclopedia, or the Chamber of Commerce booklets on most small cities can panoply a startling array of churches. Presumably they are made up of people who have somewhat different views of the ultimate reality. If they agreed, they would no doubt have merged into common units. Or, since the grasp of the ultimate does not always differ all that much, the life styles are highly varied and tensions could result. Especially when there are occasions for conflict, one would expect eruptions. Thus when in 1967 Israel was involved with a Six-Day War, not all Christians came to its defense in the face of what could have been a war to extinction. Relations were strained, but most Jews and Christians did not break them off and they have subsequently begun to rebuild them.

What has bred this tolerance in America? Some would say that if America were made up of two or three religious groups there would have been jihads or crusades, holy wars and bloody battles. But having two or three hundred groups and much mobility between them assures a certain limited potential to conflict. If concord or understanding broke down the United States would see not warfare but the law of the jungle. The openness of the religious communities is another factor. That is, through mixed marriage, a constant flow of conversions, resettlements as people move from place to place, the arbitrary way some people decide on their affiliations, the lines between most groups never harden.

America has still more going for it. The separation of religious and civil realms and the disestablishment of the churches work to prevent anyone from getting the sword. Even where a religious bloc may dominate in voting—as in a largely Southern Baptist city or a northern urban Irish set of wards—citizens are too far removed from seats of power and too unmotivated to grasp the sword and carry out formal sanctions against the defeated, as their forefathers might have done. Cynics may also say that Americans are tolerant simply because they do not give a damn, they are half-believers in all religions including their own. The historic record is not clear on that; there have been fanatics and tenacious people who are anything but casual about their faith. But they have learned to see something in the viewpoints of others.

The people who shaped this nation two centuries ago

were aware of how unproductive religious battles had been in biblical times. They might appreciate the biblical record and saw themselves in its outlines, but ordinarily did not feel that they were to be God's instruments for eliminating those who disagreed with them ultimately. They knew the history of the crusades and found little that was edifying in them. Their sacred books, like John Foxe's *Book of Martyrs,* told of sufferings of Protestants at the hands of Catholics. But instead of seeking revenge, most of them were weary about enforced faiths. They might ostracize or banish a dissenter, but they were not inspired to wage war on most of their competitive colonies. Those who reached these shores had often undergone persecution in Europe. While having experienced suffering is no guarantee that people will never inflict hardship on others, and while the record of persecution is not wholly unstained, most of them had learned their lesson. They might establish a church in a colony but then, except in rare instances, they would move on and—in their own words—"connive" with dissenters to help them find freedom without disrupting the approved order.

A view of today's scene shows how well those lessons have been learned. First of all, in the explicitly denominational sense of the term, there are or have been few dead bodies. While religion has intensified other ugly conflicts in America, including the Civil War, the relations between whites and American Indians or blacks, the issues between political lefts and rights or economic classes, denominations themselves produce few dead bodies. A Freemason may have been done in by the pious in the nineteenth century. Joseph Smith, the founder of the Mormons, was martyred, and some corpses were on the scene in Utah's "Mormon War," which had to do more with law and boundary than with religious tenets. If some Catholics were killed by Protestants, without denying the power of religious symbols it must also be noted that much of the tension had to do with ethnicity, immigration, and not creeds. And given the intensity of Protestant distaste for Catholic (European) views of American freedom, the fears that these be transported to the United States, and the inflaming rhetoric, it is astonishing to see how little rioting and bloodshed there was.

If there are no dead bodies, so there is a tolerance to the advertising slogans about American religious options. People can deride the idea of going to "the church of your choice," as if such decisions are as arbitrary as the choice of service stations, haberdashers, and supermarkets. But behind the pitch or the hype is a more profound idea: that this nation allows extensive freedom of choice without threat to the social fabric. And this freedom implies respect for people who have made other choices. On many levels, then, even before ecumenical movements and brotherhood groups were available, people had some sense that alternatives were conceivable. They may not go to the Lord's Supper or share a *seder* with others, but they might enjoy the Presbyterian strawberry festival, even if they were Catholic and they might buy a chance for a Catholic lottery even if they did not share Catholic faith.

One of the creative ways in which Americans have faced their interfaith problems has been through humor. In finding something funny about other people's view of ultimate reality or religious practice, they set themselves up for gaining some distance on their own. The great writers who kept alive the comic vision in America, among them Mark Twain, regularly twitted the religious. Church people have always been a bit nervous about such writing, but they have read it with fascination, since humorists tend to have leveling or egalitarian tendencies. Sooner or later all groups will have something to be offended about—or will have some reason for chuckling about themselves.

Given the passion with which Americans have characteristically seen their nation as being religious, it is also impressive to note how little overt hostility there has been against public anti-religion. True, anti-religious people have had an instinct by which they took refuge in low visibility. The American Association for the Advancement of Atheism on the national level has probably never been as powerful as a single small town Rotary or Lions club. Many of the humanist associations have been impotent, born obsolete, and beside the point. But America has seen significant agnostic expressions, particularly in higher academies, and yet people send their children to these schools. When the "infidel" celebrity of various eras came to town, the pious did not stone him. They bought lecture tickets and bragged about the fact that they had exposed themselves to his offerings.

A Robert Ingersoll could thus sell tickets to the Presbyterians and be a safe Republican political supporter, and Mark Twain, for all his ribaldry and blasphemy, was absorbed into the circles of acceptibility. No atheist died for his faith; few agnostics were ostracized for their unconventionality.

Similarly, most Americans have accepted the rules of the game in which the Supreme Court asks for the civil society to be "wholesomely neutral" in matters religious. It may be true that now and then some militant group may consider its particular tenets to be universal. Thus some Southern Baptists may think that because they find gambling to be wrong everyone must. Or Roman Catholics may consider their views of abortion to be "natural law" that has to be supported by all true Americans. Yet no one "takes his bat and ball and goes home." Civil society survives despite differences of this profound character.

Wherever there has been a danger that relations break down, generous people—usually lay persons—have done what they could to minimize conflict. The various "brotherhood" organizations like the National Conference of Christians and Jews have been effective in their efforts to bring together people who could produce conflict, were no provision for interaction made. People may make fun of the superficialities of "brotherhood week" but the thoughtful know they are bene-

ficiaries of those who made religious toleration a positive goal in pluralist America.

Similarly, gestures individual people and small
groups make can be derided because they do not represent complete solutions. However, they often represent subtle behavioral patterns of the kind that make
life livable. In Milwaukee, Wisconsin, a number of
Jews have for some years volunteered to take the place
of Christian bartenders on Christmas Eve. That may
seem to be empty and to the nondrinking Americans a
kind of semireligious move full of ambiguity and
moral complication. But to those who live in the Milwaukee ethos it is a way of saying, "We may not agree
with you, but we know how important your way is to
you—and that is important to us." When a Christian
church burns and a synagogue invites the congregation
to share space, an important symbol is enacted that
transcends ideology.

If we have concentrated on behavioral gestures and
policies unsupported by dogmas, it is also important
not to overlook the place of philosophies of toleration.
Through the years Christians, Jews, and people not
in the biblical heritage, have devised ways in which
they could both advocate their particular visions and
hold a regard for other people's faiths. Sometimes
these creeds are presented in popular fashion: "We are
all in different boats heading for the same shore." But
such sentiments can also be grounded in profound approaches. Thus Father John Courtney Murray, speaking for a most thoughtful Catholicism, said that pluralism may be against the will of God (who is truth,

and is one), but it is written into the cards of history and will not suddenly stop troubling the human city.

All these present-day efforts have long roots in history. The achievement of religious toleration is all the more remarkable for the fact that few had come to seek it. Europeans in the seventeenth century, long after the Protestant Reformation, were still trying to settle conflicts with power and the sword. Not until the Glorious Revolution of 1688 were the British, the main ancestors of American institutions, beginning to foresee glimmers of modern-day toleration. Americans had few precedents; they knew what they did not like and could not endure.

The arrangements on these shores were by no means born of a desire for toleration. Lord Baltimore in Maryland, as a spokesman for a Catholic minority, had to settle for it. William Penn, who believed in it and who also believed that given time the spirit would lead every one to see truth as he saw it, allowed for it and assured it in Pennsylvania. Virginian Anglicanism was relatively tolerant, though there were bad moments. But in New England the colonists planned to know nothing but homogeneity within any colony. Dissenters were free—to go elsewhere.

Toleration came when people saw that persecution and repression did not work. The price for religious uniformity was too high in freedoms that the colonists did cherish. The call for mutual understanding was reinforced both by religious groups that were not in command in colonies (like Quakers and Baptists) and by the enlightened statesmen, enemies of sectarianism.

So ideals of toleration have both Christian and non-Christian roots. Most of all, the practical situation had its effects. Church historian Philip Schaff said that Americans were "shut up" to the course they took, if they wanted one nation to grow out of the many establishments.

The nineteenth century saw tests of the new resolves, as Roman Catholics—whose European counterparts were busy expressing themselves in terms inimical to American governmental liberties—came by the millions and as Jews made their presence felt in numbers. Somehow, despite struggle and conflict, the American way began to work. In the twentieth century the idea of pluralism was still hard for the old majorities to swallow. But swallow it they did in a retreat or a yielding seldom experienced by dominant majorities. The Protestants could probably have held on to their old power much longer than they did. Something in their vision, something not as negative as apathy and not always as positive as wholehearted assent, led them to join with others in promoting the understanding that America could both assure people a grasp on the ultimate and the ability to live with those who had other grasps and goals.

- 6 -

A Promised Land for All Races

WHILE AMERICANS have shown impressive progress in overcoming religious differences, it must be said that in the modern world other kinds of divisions between people have represented knottier problems. Religion does not amount to enough to assure people that they can give full expression to their hates and prejudices by sniping at each other across the lines of faith. Modern nationalism is much more potent; millions die in wars over the boundaries on which it depends. Perhaps even more terrifying and mystifying is the ability race has to draw people into conflict.

Why, it may be asked, bring the topic of race into a book on American religiousness at all? Should it not properly be dealt with by students of humankind in anthropology, scholars of social relations in sociology, psychology, or history? It should be dealt with, should it not, by social workers, politicians, and experts in intergroup relations. What does race have to do with

the spiritual forces? Those questions might make
sense in a world removed from real people. But anyone who has become familiar with the way people
make up their minds about reality has to know that race
and faith are connected in astonishing ways.

Maybe someday people will know more about the
physical differences between races than we do now;
they will speak with more assurance than people now
can about different psychological make-ups of those
who derive from Africa, Asia, or the West. But at
present little seems to be known, and the unknown
regularly calls forth religious explanations. Most races
have mythic and symbolic explanations of how they
came to be and how they came to be different from
others. Creator gods left the black man in their ovens
too long, and the whites too briefly, but the reds were
prepared just right; it would take little guessing to
know that a "red man" is telling the story that way.

In American Christianity, for example, where white
religion dominated, somehow or other the ruling people came to the conclusion that blacks were descendants
of Noah's cursed son, Ham, and that by a divine principle they could be enslaved to burden-bearing cast.
The Bible gave not a hint of the color of Ham and
made nothing of this "curse" in its later references to
black people. But white racists needed nothing more to
go on. These myths are not merely harmless stories
passed on from parents to children. Social institutions
embody the results of such storytelling, and people act
irrationally on the basis of them.

In the field of race, two good rules could apply: if

you would like to stimulate racism, be sure to associate religious symbols with your explanations and prejudices.

Conversely, should you wish to improve relations between races, be sure to associate the changes with divine mandates and explanations. Speak of how people are all of one blood—as the Bible does—and of how a faith unites people across racial boundaries; this the Bible also does. American religion has seen much application of both rules. Given its special problems, it is noteworthy to see the regular part religion has played in helping overcome racial differences. No one pretends that the American record is what it should be, given the white majority's dealings with American Indians or with Negroes. Nor should reciprocal racism on the part of minorities be overlooked in anyone's doctrine of man as it is lived out in the United States.

The bad record can be qualified, however, by reference to the special problems each generation of Americans inherits from its predecessors. Seldom in history has one nation found itself faced with so many races living near each other. During the colonial and early national period the conquering whites and the Indians lived near each other. Since land was at issue, it was inevitable that there would be clashes. Whites can be faulted for having enslaved imported blacks, but later generations who were not responsible for such policies found themselves living in countless southern villages and later northern suburbs; they were pushed near races they did not understand but with which they had to compete and which they had to explain.

Given the problems then of being embarked on a relatively tight ship together and having no choice but to begin to coexist, Americans have made some gains and religion has regularly been a factor. While the poem in the Statue of Liberty evokes no special divine invitation when it welcomes the world's poor, tired, huddled masses, the people who received these masses worked hard to find religious explanations for their presence and purpose and eventually for positive relations to them. While the differences were more often ethnic than racial, nineteenth-century people spoke of northern and southern Europeans or eastern and western Europeans as being of different races. In their eyes, Jews clearly belonged to a different racial stock. For some years Orientals poured onto Western shores, adding still another surprising element in the racial mix. In the middle of the twentieth century, Caribbean peoples of different ethnic backgrounds made their way in an airborne migration. America kept on inviting problems and kept on finding solutions.

One of the best proofs that America has faced the mystery and the brute facts of race fairly creatively can be seen in the recognition that, once here, most people want to stay. They used to tell the story of an Italian immigrant woman who wept on her tenement doorstep. "Why are you crying?" "Because I want to go back to Italy?" "Why, then, did you come to America?" "To raise enough money to go back to Italy." Some did return to Europe, often becoming aliens in their old homelands in the process. But most stayed and most wanted to. The old Afro-European and sometimes Asiatic homelands remained as beckoning symbols. We always thought we *could* escape if the going got rough. But we knew that we did not really want to go.

An illustration of these attitudes shows up in the many religiously based "back to Africa" movements. Long before militants spoke of a return in the 1960s, black churches were producing people who like Henry McNeal Turner called forth images as a Christian of "an African kingdom of God." But few blacks responded, and they developed religious and even biblical imagery about a Promised Land in America—a good sign that they were not only content with being here as opposed to somewhere else, but even that they saw promise for a future here. When Jews came in the nineteenth century many of them would talk the language of Zionism in relation to Israel. But just as many more began to say that "America is our Zion, our Jerusalem," and few left.

All this means that the racial groups staked out a claim on American soil and then undertook a course of action that helped them express hopes in religious terms; that the whites did so with their talk about "manifest destiny" and "mission" was always noticed. That almost everyone else did is a fact coming more and more to light.

So positive and so rich in opportunity has the American environment appeared to be that racial groups have taken pains constantly to improvise new solutions depending upon circumstances—and to find religious warrant for doing so. To take but one recent example that is quite vivid to people: if the legend about Ham's curse dominated many black-white relations, the time came when other religious symbols were associated with racial integration. Martin Luther King, for example, regularly used biblical language to speak of amity and concord; most of his power came from the fact that biblical symbols could be used by people of good will on both sides of old racial walls. When races entered new stages of separation, they employed religious symbols (from Africa, from a re-reading of the Bible and history) to justify the stepping back from integration. And when they offered longer-range pictures of coming together again, these were usually religious. They would talk about God's coming kingdom.

American religionists have contributed to a constantly improving legal situation for racial minorities. While it is a truism to say that around 1954 the courts began to drag Americans screaming into a new era, the religious groups immediately revised their approaches and often set the pace. And historians can show how the seeds had been widely dispersed by people of spiritual outlook long before the courts began to harvest them. Some people said that the churches needed the racial-integration and civil rights movements more than these movements needed the churches. But few could deny that churches played very important parts in bringing about change. Thus when the Congress passed extensive civil rights legislation in 1964, both those who admired the churches' involvements and those who hated such activity paid the religious forces a compliment when they pointed to their intense and broad contributions.

If that was true in the 1950s or 1960s, so it has been throughout American history. The early Quakers were among the first to work for abolition of slavery and improvement of the conditions of American blacks. Evangelicals led in the abolition movements; however much resistance they met from other Christians who wanted slavery and segregation, these abolitionists often moved on specifically Christian grounds of inspiration and interpretation. Were one to prepare a textbook that anthologized and collected the historical sources on improving race relations, a significant portion of the pages would have to include religious leaders from Anthony Benezet and John Woolman down through antislavery leaders to Martin Luther King and his lesser-known white counterparts. They related religion to law, to good effect. The condition of southern blacks has demonstrably improved in recent years as a result. While people regularly say that you cannot legislate morality, they have shown that they can legislate a change in circumstances so that new moral conditions can emerge.

If American believers have seldom done all that they should have to change the circumstances, they have been more reachable on religious grounds than on almost any other when it comes to the issue of recognizing faults, piercing consciences, and working toward new resolves.

Religion played its part in helping oppressed races come to terms with and then transcend their conditions. Where there could not be concord between races, there was not, at least, always despair within each racial circle. If whites systematically deprived blacks of their African religions, the new faiths they passed on were appropriated in special ways by the blacks who used them to prophesy and depict hopes for the future. Many of the later-arriving racial groups found opportunity in America that they had not known elsewhere. Religion played an important part, for instance, in building Jewish community in America. Whatever experiences of anti-Semitism Jews here have known, they know that almost nowhere else are there better grounds for creative Jewish existence than in the American environment of interactions.

Even where there have been barriers along racial lines, expressions of good will have been inspired by religious impulses. Many who join organizations like the National Conference of Christians and Jews or the National Association for the Advancement of Colored People do so because their religious faith motivates them; many who undertake controversial missions such as the support of Chicano migratory workers are inspired by their vision of what God calls them to do. The most supportive white group for American Indian self-assertion has been made up of church people.

Throughout these pages there has been a complicating undertone. It is not difficult to show that religious forces spent decades if not centuries rediscovering the roots of their heritages, roots which would issue in racial concord and integration. Yet in recent years religion has also been employed to justify new separation on the part of minorities. Is not this an embarrassment? The answer to such a question has to do with how one regards the short-range and long-range goals and changes necessary. At one stage, for example, Christian blacks in America clung to the integrationist models also for the short range, believing that through them they could best realize the fulfillment of their divinely inspired intentions. When they discovered that realization could not easily come because they were being integrated into someone else's America or some-one else's church they stepped back.

At such a stage they reached into their own racially derived myths and symbols for reinterpretation as they sought power, identity, manhood, and womanhood. Few of them have deserted the vision of a human family, but they have had to defer the dream. Most of them would argue that such deferment is also accompanied by religious explanations. On these grounds, too, religion's role should not be overlooked.

So long as the American Indian was nothing but an object for Christian mission he could be misused and could become a subject for extinction or removal. But when the Indian's own religious self-assertion became comprehensible to non-Indian majorities, his status was more secure and his voice was heard. Vine Deloria in *Custer Died for Your Sins* and *We Talk, You Listen* symbolizes this Indian assertiveness and he and his colleagues have begun to gain hearings.

So long as black destiny was in the hands of non-blacks entirely and so long as these largely white gentile people could redefine them through religious symbols, it was hard for blacks to find their true place in America. When they reached into biblical or African religious materials, or when they transformed the religion imparted to them as slaves into a more revolutionary way of explaining their black power and black beauty, they made possible a fresh appraisal of their ways in America. It is not improbable that out of this appraisal will come a more durable model of interaction and some sort of integration than was earlier envisioned.

So long as Jews were sequestered in Gentile-produced ghetto walls they could be "Christ-killers" or whatever. But when they interpreted the European Holocaust and the rise of Israel in biblical and other religious terms and asserted their role afresh, they were regarded more seriously than ever before. So it has been with most of the immigrant groups—the people of various ethnic backgrounds or races. The drama is not finished, but significant acts have been played.

-7-

An Expressive Laity

RELIGION is not supposed to touch only the lives of the few. In primitive and religious cultures it was assumed that everyone in a society would be religious and would share the same religion. In the Christian world, it is never hinted that Jesus Christ died and rose only for a professional few. He gave himself for all, and all who are called to be his and who are called by his name are expected to take on a full range of privilege and responsibility in his church.

While all are implicated in religion, then, it has always happened that a division has grown between leaders and followers. In primitive societies this would be most obvious. What was everybody's job was nobody's job. So someone in particular would lead the dance or say the prayers or be the witchdoctor. This person would come to such a status by heritage and inheritance; or even by casting of lots or some other random method he or she would acquire leadership status. Sometimes this person would have a "charism," a natural gift that would mark him for such a role.

The larger populace would be a largely passive support group for whom services would be performed.

In the modern world the old distinctions between priest and nonpriest lived on. Such a survival is not necessarily bad. It might still be said that what is everyone's job is no one's job, and that it is advantageous to set aside a special group of people—perhaps even having been set aside by a divine call. But the modern world has also seen a great growth in the potential and the capability of the nonleader, nonprofessional, or lay group. This is all to the good, since religious power increases geometrically when so many well-poised, equipped, and well-located men and women can share in extending the purposes and services of a religious group.

Even the definitions of clergy and lay relations have changed in the modern world. Most Protestant groups have been concerned to find new ways to indicate that lay people are full sharers in the divine life as expressed in religious organizations. They are not to be second-class citizens on a lower plane. Much is made of the fact that the Protestant Reformation removed the old clergy/lay caste system and liberated lay people for full service. The idea of "the priesthood of all believers" is often thought of as characteristic of Protestantism.

Modern Catholicism has also democratized its definitions. Some inherited descriptions made the church essentially a hierarchy of clergy, with lay people serving them and being served. But the Second Vatican Council in numerous documents talked lavishly about lay responsibility and freedom; indeed, in most places where the church was to go into the world, the lay people alone were free to go.

What, it might be asked, has any or all of this to do with the celebration of religion in the American Bicentennial? The answers to such a question have their roots in the record of lay development in American life. For a couple of hundred years, in most places, clergy occupied no special legal privilege as managers of the established church in America. Perhaps in part because of the separation of civil and religious realms the clergy formed no "sitting target." Hence there was less occasion for anticlericalism and lay people were free to develop positively, without so much negative reference to a clerical caste supported by people who did not share their beliefs. Here in America the levels and standards of education have been high, so lay people have been well equipped. Here religious organizations take special pains to train nonclerics in the mysteries of faith and religious action. In the wide pluralism of American life lay leaders can easily develop their various kinds of talents, since few pre-cut patterns inhibit them. Much has been expected of American nonprofessionals in religion. They have had opportunities, and many have taken advantage of these.

The Protestant background of so much American religion helped it in this respect. Roman Catholics were long inhibited by sacramental views that elevated clergy at the expense of laity. But Protestants had developed the idea that before God all Christians were equal: the mother washing diapers or preparing a meal, the humble plowman, or mechanic were, in God's eyes at least, on a par with the monk mumbling his prayers or the preacher preparing his sermon. Since all thirteen colonies were largely Protestant at the time the nation was formed, American religionists were more or less programmed not to be inhibited by old Catholic ideas.

Today one can explore all the corners of American religious life and see lay initiative. In the newer religious groups, the communes and occult cults, there are leaders but they do not ordinarily have inherited and traditional rules that define their clerical status. In local congregations the American tradition, particularly in Judaism and in Protestantism, allows for and expects a great deal of democratic lay participation.

The polity of most churches indicates just how true this is in formal terms. A characteristic American development in church government was the congregational pattern. This was strong not only in colonial Congregationalism and its heirs, but among the tens of millions later members of all kinds of Baptist, Disciples of Christ, Christian, and Church of Christ circles. In Congregationalism a clerical leadership survived, of course. But this form of church life always implied a great deal of consultation with and debate on the part of lay persons. In effect, they called and could dismiss pastors, and leaders were accountable to them, while no outside force stood or stands in their way.

The congregational and essentially laic spirit lives on far beyond churches of that polity. In Presbyterianism the lay people as elders (presbyters) have important say in determining policy; the Episcopalians have a House of Deputies in their governance; Lutherans make much of their presbygational patterns. Where there is no official form of lay dominance of clerical choice and pattern, unofficially lay people often find ways to be consulted. Thus in Methodism the bishop theoretically could act against the will of the people in the placing of ministers, but few bishops would be so ill-advised as not to be responsive.

Major efforts are made to give lay people room to express themselves. Denominational periodicals, still given too much to reporting on people who wear clerical collars, now also compete to find unusual, outstanding, or representative lay men and women expressing their faith in their vocations. Or others will take pains to assign roles to lay people that once looked clerical. There are laymen's Sundays, which could be condescending tokens were it not also true that in such churches lay people preach more and more frequently. Adult Christian higher education is one of several means of equipping lay people to carry on acts of ministry. In fact, almost every kind of effort for church renewal concentrates on equipping the whole people of God to be the people of God. Honest efforts are thus made to de-clericalize religion.

Judaism represents a special kind of case. In Jewish concepts there is technically speaking no clergy at all. The rabbi is in a sense the teacher, a leader who has not been set aside for priestly roles. But it happened that in a largely Christian environment Judaism looked more and more clericalized. Yet in recent years efforts have been made by Jews to return to their earlier concepts. And all the while it must be said that while rabbis were coming to seem more like priests and ministers in their roles, the lay initiative never died out. In many respects the synagogue is lay-run. Even more important, Jewish lay people have found countless instruments for service in the world as representatives of the Jewish vision, either through or in spite of the synagogue.

For a couple of hundred years lay people have found a special outlet for their talents in the network of agencies designed for service in the world. There are leagues or orders of lay persons, men and women, in almost every religious group. In a democratic society people take it for granted that denominational conventions will not be clerically dominated.

Entirely apart from formal ecclesiastical life lay people have found ways to speak out of their faith contexts in many worlds. If theologians have been largely confined to clerical ranks, some of the most notable interpreters of American religious life have been lay persons—some of them barely connected with the churches. Thus one thinks of Abraham Lincoln, who did not feel at home as a member in any denomination. Yet his speeches reflect the spirit of someone who constantly brooded on and expounded biblical themes as these took shape in the life of the national community. The poets and prophets of America have often been lay people, many of them not really at home in the conventional religious groups but still expressive of religious visions: Ralph Waldo Emerson, William James, Emily Dickinson are names that come to mind at once.

In political life laity have been especially expressive. From the beginning, a significant percentage of political leaders have without embarrassment dedicated their energies to living out of the ethical resources of their faith. Of course it is true that politicians know that it may be popular and profitable to exploit religion and to sound pious. But just as often they have acted without much reference to popularity and have even inconvenienced themselves by trying to act congruently with religious visions. These are also not necessarily churchly looking expressions, but they show that without benefit of clergy Americans have continued to give laity a chance to be free for service in the world.

The voice of followers-as-leaders or of lay persons is not just a recent phenomenon. In colonial times the opportunities were already there. It is impressive to see how much of the leadership of the colonies was in actuality and in outlook lay dominated. This is true despite the fact that the seventeenth-century world was normally and instinctively much more clerical than our own, and also despite the fact that clerics in those days tended to be rather formidable figures who were more than ready to assert themselves.

From the long corridor formed by decades of history the colonies looked more clericalized than they actually were. Nowadays historians are getting back to the long neglected records. In a typical account of a New England village's history we find a lay person saying to his cleric that, his office aside, the layman respected the minister no more than any other person. Many of the leaders of religion were actually governors, elders, and councilmen. While today's world remembers the clerical Cottons and Mathers, it also recalls that Governor Bradford and other nonordained people marked the days and events of their colonies from the viewpoint of the Bible and their church's teachings.

In part, lay people had a chance to develop because there was a chronic undersupply of clergy. In many settings the rites and orders of the church could not be acted upon were it not for the activity of lay persons. They usually welcomed clergy on the scene; their theology was not always ready for sacramental life or even preaching to be undertaken without reference to clergy. But they had to improvise, and they actually engaged in many undefined borderline activities. When clerics came, they did not yield all of these lightly.

One other factor for lay participation was the "low church" character of so much early American religion. Quakers like William Penn and others were thoroughly lay in their outlook and were suspicious of anything that looked like clericalism; yet they performed functions that looked ministerial.

A great impetus toward the laicization of America came from the people who helped form the nation apart from positive references to the churches just two centuries ago. Most of these were not overtly antichurch, though many of them were only nominal members and even more expressed uncertainty about or criticism of clericalism and church establishment. "My own mind is my church," said Thomas Paine, one of the more radical of these. Much of Jefferson's attack was against "priestcraft" or clericalism. In the Jefferson Monument today's Sunday school children still look up to read the huge encircling inscription that tells of Jefferson's eternal hostility to every form of tyranny over the minds of man. Little do most of them know that he was complaining about the clergy in that sentence.

These vestrymen and elders of their churches took religion out of the sanctuary and brought it into the public forum where lay religion has always thrived. Today's scholars like to talk about a "religion of the republic" or a civil or societal religion. When they do so they are often making reference to faiths that were generated right under the noses of clerics when these ministers did not move rapidly enough to face changes that a free society induced or produced.

The years of the "evangelical empire" in the century after the nation was formed saw a great expansion of lay initiative. While denominations and clergy eventually tended to take them over, most of the humanitarian and missionary organizations early in the century were ecumenical and lay-directed. The often derided American system of "joiners" in voluntary associations grew out of lay inventiveness in church circles. The lay people were often close to the poor, and they worked to change their circumstances. They knew how deprived of religious ministry many were, and took direct action to supply them with Bibles, tracts, the spoken word, and a helping hand.

For peculiar historical reasons, Roman Catholicism was not in those periods as free to see lay people fulfill themselves as was Judaism, Protestantism, or were the many new sects and cults that grew up at the margins of established churches. While many of these later turned clerical, they often were the voice of people who were not content with the ways their own clergy had set forth. And today Catholicism and virtually all groups allow freedom seldom before dreamed of in religious history for lay involvement.

-8-

The Progressive
Liberation of Women

HISTORY IS the story of men and women struggling to breathe free. By no means is it always a success story. The twentieth century has seen more people executed or held captive behind barbed wire and stockades than any previous time. In most parts of the world people cannot say what they think or be what they would want to be without fear of punishment by a repressive and dominating class. Nations try to subjugate nations, castes oppress other castes, classes war against classes. Few people are free to live out their creative potential.

If history has had many sad and tragic turns, it has also seen its brighter moments. In the Western world, for example, slavery has been abolished almost everywhere. Ancient and apparently timeless customs and practices died in the nineteenth century. Various minority races have found new freedom in the contexts of majority cultures. For all the limitations, American blacks, for example, are certainly in better circumstances than they were a century ago. Wage slavery still exists, but the organization of labor has brought new dignity to millions who in the earlier stages of industrial revolutions had no means of speaking for themselves. Franchises have been fought for and extended to new classes of people in nation after nation. Developing or "Third World" nations are assertive, having largely cast off colonial bindings and yokes. Political and civil liberties are broader than before.

The rise of modern women's movements must be seen in the context of these struggles. The quest for women's liberation is not isolated. This is especially true so far as the question of religion is concerned. All of the revolutions and strivings have religious dimensions. They tend to involve theological views of how the universe is put together, what the gods intended for humans, how affairs were to be ordered. Religious institutions have often been cast on both sides of the battles. Here again, the quest for freedom, equality, and dignity by women has been no exception.

The roots of sexual attitudes are as mysterious as are those that have to do with roots of racism. They lie deep in hidden historical experiences and in fundamental grasps of reality on the part of primitive people. When the great religions of the world took rise, they addressed these mysteries, and myths or symbols accounting for the hopes and fears associated with men's and women's sexual nature and status were stamped deep on the minds of individuals and in the practices of cultures.

The New World was discovered and colonized and by the time the American nation was founded two centuries ago, no one could "start from scratch." These ingrained attitudes could not easily be abolished. But the American centuries have seen great progress. And if women still have a long, long way to go, they can credit their religion for playing some part in their liberation—including freedom from bad religious attitudes.

Most of the new religions in America, whether in their nineteenth-century forms (Christian Science, the New Thought movements, para-Christian cults, and sects) or in the mid-twentieth century, when communalism and Eastern religions made their way, have included women among the pioneers and developers. But the major and more durable tests and styles of progress occur within the setting of America's majority religion, which derives from the Bible.

The Bible, fortunately or unfortunately, cannot easily be exhausted or easily cited on one side of modern political and humanistic issues. It is a record of God's dealing with humans through many centuries and in varied circumstances. Seldom can its dealings be translated into literal applications for modern life (e.g., shall I be Republican or Democrat; must I support or oppose this Fair Housing Law over against another version?) For that reason biblical religion has had representatives on both sides of the women-and-religion issue.

Radical feminists, including those in religious circles, have plenty of opportunity to find what are to them embarrassing texts in the Bible and, even more, in the traditions that ensue from it. Almost all the church fathers and male heroes of the Christian and Jewish past were shaped by their male-dominated cultures and they naturally turned to the biblical lore that justified their prejudices and claims. Ruling groups do not lightly yield power, and men ruled. Therefore these religious men can be made to look silly because, by our later lights, they were silly in the way they saw women and because of the self-confidence with which they tied God to their own vision of things.

Biblical religion has another side, however. While it is true that the pronouns associated with deity are masculine, there are many feminine motifs in the Bible. The *shekinah* or "showing forth of God's presence" is feminine; the Virgin Mary has been an object of adoration or a subject of devotion in the majority of Christianity; the People of God and the church are often referred to in the feminine gender. The Hebrew Scriptures show women as prophetesses who spoke for Yahweh, and were expressive servants of his. In the New Testament, while no women were in the symbolic band of twelve disciples, they assume responsible places in the proclamation of the kingdom. They were the announcers of Christ's resurrection. They appeared dignified and alert when the disciples were often seen as frail and pathetic.

In St. Paul's letters women are often seen in leadership positions in the church, though Paul never seemed to make up his mind just what part they should play. He could tell the Corinthians that when women prophesied or prayed they should keep their heads covered—and then turn around in the same letter and have them not prophesying at all! Christian history has seen its women saints by the hundreds, its mystics by the dozens. But these were always seen as exceptions until modern times.

The unfolding has come in recent centuries. It cannot be said that America always pioneers. Many European nations, for example, have led in the ordination of women to the ministry. But overall, Americans have played major parts in the religious side of women's liberation. Nor are all expressions of women's creativity to be seen in the context of the liberating struggle. A perception of American religion finds women responsibly involved on almost every level.

The local congregation is one good test. While one may rue the fact that so few ordained clerics in most churches are women, in every other respect they tend to be leaders. They make up the majority of congregations and, in many cases, the majority of congregational leadership. Even though more and more of them have joined work forces outside the home, they have not lost their capacity for volunteering in various ac tivities. Almost any denominational periodical showing women's participation in religion exemplifies that part professional women play. Not all of these activities represent passive women, being submissive to dominant male authority. The radical feminists sometimes see church activities as distractions from what they consider to be valid battles, but women in church life find great fulfillment there. Despite frustrations, they are not always angry, not always waiting for movements to come to perfection before they take up with them.

The matter of leadership has been changing in America, as well. Seventy-five denominations now ordain women and these women are gradually overcoming male and female prejudices as they undertake ever broader tasks and find higher status. A symbol of frustration has been the practice of ordination, a formal sanctioning for clerical office. Today's women either shrug off the idea of ordination, or they become ordained; in either case, they are not content merely to join a well-defined elite. They want to redefine the terms of ministry and its tasks. Women more and more frequently become elected presidents of denominations, ecumenical forces, and the like.

In Roman Catholicism the issue is as confused as in Protestantism. Catholicism long had outlets for women that Protestantism did not have in religious orders of sisters. The old ethos in these orders was full of submissiveness to religiously dominant males. But since the Vatican Council of 1962–65 those women who stayed in religious orders have been among the most assertive speakers for women's rights in religious circles.

Theologically everything is opening up. Not everyone is as angry as some of the feminists. Many of them are sophisticated about the contexts of the past and know how to "overcome history with history." But more and more of them are also engaging in a critical reappraisal of the Scriptures of various religions. They are asking the churches to allow the latent liberating elements in the Bible—including the writings of St. Paul—to be heard in our times. They do not try to explain away the apparently repressive texts, but they argue that Paul's vision "in Christ there is neither male nor female" was a picture of a future into which the church is to grow.

As far as outreach is concerned, much of this remains chiefly in the hands of women. They head the forces of teachers, who decisively shape a new generation. When these women are freed from old stereotypes, they pass on a message of fulfillment and freedom. They are the deaconesses and nurses and, as they have for decades, they have taken leading parts in the missionary activities. The day is long past when the only influential women in the church were parson's wives, whose influence had to be subtle and indirect. "Consciousness-altering" is going on, as can be seen or heard in the changes of terminologies of church constitutions (where male-dominant language is disappearing) and in the language of the liturgy. The cleric who arises in front of a majority of women and begins, "Dear brethren in Christ . . . " will expect to be dismissed as a relic of a more thoughtless time.

The changes have occurred against the background of a very ambiguous history of religion in America. There is little ambiguity or mystery about the first two centuries in the English colonies. The history books have little to do with women at all. They show up now and then as ministers' wives, in whose orbits of influence they made their own impacts. Today we are coming to recognize as heroines the few who in their own time were dismissed as heretics. Modern Americans are more sympathetic toward the Quaker and Anabaptist women who seemed to go out of their way to provoke authorities in their own time—all in the interests not of women's rights but of "soul liberty" for everyone.

The story of what women endured and overcame will be told progressively as new techniques of historical writing come into play and as people retrace the sources. The women's liberation movement and historians of town and family are discerning more and more of the plot concerning women in early America —a story that had been overlooked simply because so many chroniclers have concentrated only on what the establishment did. Women were not then part of the establishment.

It must also be said that the people whose memory a nation recalls at bicentennial time did little for women. The statesmen who draughted the fundamental documents of the American tradition talked about rights, but granted few to women or slaves. This might seem like a strange point to bring up in a chapter devoted to the positive relations between the growth of women's rights and American religion. Yet the tradition of the Enlightenment is often seen as the true liberator, while "church religion" has been dismissed as suppressive of freedom.

The bases of women's movements in America did not derive so much from "the religion of the republic," though its logic was eventually to be of help. It grew in the wonderful tangle of nineteenth-century religious movements. While the story is not one of sudden and dramatic victories, it is true that at almost every turn during that century, women were present and active. Perhaps the most representative movement of the times was the missionary activity. An expansive evangelical America sent missionaries into all the world. Women were at first kept at home in supportive roles. But beginning in 1800 they began to organize, to send, to go. It would be impossible to tell the story of the nineteenth-century global movement without having about as many women's names in the index as men's.

If allowing women to go overseas might look as if male America were merely exiling women and confining them to very nonrevolutionary activity, their role in more controversial spheres can be noted. In the whole matter of the liberation of slaves, women like the Grimké sisters of South Carolina and Harriet Beecher Stowe of *Uncle Tom's Cabin* fame were leaders. The humanitarian agencies were often staffed and inspired by women. In that period of what Alice Felt Tyler called "Freedom's Ferment," many religiously based communes or communities were founded. Not a few of the leaders were charismatic women. The transmission of religious faith to a new generation is one of the most decisive things a believing people can do. In the course of the century this activity came to be more and more in the hands of women, as was public education, a sphere where the formation of values on religious grounds played such an important role in personal and national life.

Roman Catholicism in this period did not have many famous women leaders, in part because they tended to be excluded from almost all areas of influence except the supervision of their own religious orders of sisters. Also, because most Catholics were still crammed into urban ghettos where mere survival as a minority in a strange new land gave few women the opportunity to struggle for their full rights. But the urban Jewish community, even though it represented a religion where women had not had many public responsibilities, soon produced a generation of women who pioneered in quasi-religious social welfare activities.

The feminist and suffrage forces saw that religion could be both a retarding or an enhancing force. Thus, according to Aileen Kraditor, the militant feminists often attacked both the imagery and practices of American religion. But—and this is truly significant —they often modified their attacks and turned gentle at the last minute when they discovered that ministers of religion supported their cause in larger numbers than did males of any other profession. Something was latent in the logic of biblical religion that could not leave consciences at ease. While some feminists were anti-religious, many others successfully worked to let the liberating word of religion free themselves from many old conventions and the male-dominated society from its old "ease in Zion."

Part III
The American
Experience

-9-

The Humanitarian Impulse

AMONG AMERICAN religion's most notable achievements have been its humanitarian and charitable activities. While religion can be used for people's private advancement or to justify the competitive growth of churchly institutions, it can also call forth measures of sacrifice and altruism. In the United States it has long done so.

Religions in the modern world are often judged by their effects. This has not necessarily been the case always before or everywhere. In the primitive world religion is an all-enveloping element of life; no one escapes its explanations or its rituals. Whether or not these are ethical and whether or not they issue in good deeds done for others is often beside the point. People simply "are" a part of a religious universe of discourse and they know no other way of looking at life than the way that faith provides.

Biblical religion, among others, produced a different

set of measures and results. Its prophetic strain has
regularly called people to be religious by letting their
love of God show through in their dealings with fellow
humans. How one dealt with widows and orphans,
neighbors, rivals and enemies—this was to be the new
standard of judgment. One was to do justly, love
mercy, and walk humbly with God, according to the
prophet Micah. For Jesus, not all who said "Lord,
Lord" would enter the kingdom, but rather those who
did the will of the father. Whoever passed the cup of
cold water to the child, or found Christ in the sick or
imprisoned, would be the one who would be num-
bered among those who received their rewards. Even
more, his followers were to lose themselves in self-
sacrificing love without looking for reward at all.
Their faith was to be made active in love.

Throughout Christian history this charitable note
has seldom been totally lost. While much fault can be
found with the motives and effects of "alms-giving,"
however, through long centuries alms were given in
part at least to satisfy the claims of Christ on the
human heart. Also, before America was colonized or
before the United States became a nation, a pattern
had already been established wherein most of the "welfare" departments were in the hands of religious
groups. Hospitals, centers of relief, hospices, schools,
agencies of charity were almost always in the hands
of priests, monks or nuns, lay leaders or ministers in
later Protestantism.

These charitable activities were often, in effect, sub-
sidized by the civil leaders and alms-giving was only

a little personal gravv or icing. People might have expected all this humanitarian concern to disappear in America, especially as religious and civil realms became separate. Who would pay for the ventures? Just the opposite happened. Religions in modern free societies have been characteristically more generous than they were previously. Not only have American religious groups had to pay for the existence of their institutions and support of their leadership, but they have given additionally. When Americans have been uncertain as to the grounds why they should be friendly to the churches, one of the most convincing cases they have heard has issued from a catalog of believers' good works for others.

The evidences of such humanitarianism are present in contemporary America on all hands. The scope is world wide. In the late eighteenth century in England and in what was becoming the United States a whole new approach to "doing things for God" developed among Protestant evangelicals, while similar programs were growing up in Continental and later American Catholicism. The modern world also called forth and produced Jewish philanthropy on a most impressive scale. Thus American good works, never wholly divorced but usually striving to be distinct from governmental and public policy, have been recognized everywhere. While "Marshall Plans" for relief in war-torn countries, as generous and beneficial as they may have sometimes been, could be dismissed as part of imperial politics, it has been less easy for America's enemies to see the gifts of America's common people, especially gathered in religious enclaves, as part of an expansionist plot. Too many mission hospitals were built out of love of Christ and not to extend the flag's or the dollar's sway to write these off as simply signs of American self-seeking even when self-giving.

Too many congregations have adopted overseas clinics; too many of America's moderately poor have collected pennies for the world's poor; too many people have risked their lives to share and spread the sometimes mixed benefits of improved agriculture, industry, or education to see these divorced from religious visions of sacrifice. After World War II the American support of World Council of Churches' relief programs made up a significant and probably even disproportionate part of the whole. American Jews, sometimes accused of acting out of guilty conscience for not migrating or for possessing so much wealth or merely to assure a symbol of identity, have been known in Israel as extenders of genuine gifts of love and hope.

Similarly, a prospect of today's America shows that however much secular and governmental forces play their part in helping people serve others, the religious groups have not lost their taste for or their percentage of similar efforts. When there are natural disasters, Christian people organize out of religious resources to try to aid. Sometimes they seem to be helping their own. For years journalistic critics have berated or twitted church editors for headlines such as "Eighty lives lost in tornado; no Catholic churches destroyed," or "Floods ravage the city; no Baptist property ruined." But if these editors have sometimes sounded

self-protective merely by doing accounting of properties, the public knows that the church people can often organize talent pools, can get people to join in
causes and develop their skills, and can keep alive the
vision of human need.

If churches can look beyond their needs in times of
suffering, they can also be of help to their own. This
is not an insignificant element in humanitarian endeavor, since over half of the population is on the rolls
of religious organizations. Long before a welfare society began to develop, these churches, however mea-
gerly, began to provide for their own aged or poor. In
a local congregation millions of instances go unre-
ported simply because they are so commonplace. For
example, a member needs blood transfusions. One call
to another member sets up a chain of help unmatched
in the public realm. If this story could be told more frequently, it is likely that the image of the churches could
be greatly improved in a society which often sees the
competitive and self-seeking side of religion. But most
of the story cannot be told either because it involves
personal and confidential references or because it is so
hard to grasp in its common and commonplace mani-
festations.

The hidden ministries in American religion are often
overlooked. When inventories of community resources
are drawn up, the public does not even know how to
reckon with church and synagogue. A listing of all the
kinds of family assistance and marital counseling will
normally not even mention the churches. Yet they often
serve people who are unreached by any other agencies;

they do so at little or no cost to the beneficiary; generosity and opportunities for service in precisely these spheres often serve to improve the morale of people in religious groups.

Nor should it be overlooked that humanitarian religion has produced countless recruits for secular ministry to those in need. Often a faith will give people the proper conscience and vision; then they grow frustrated over the limits or half-heartedness among fellow-believers. They leave the religious group to find others like-minded in voluntary associations or in the governmental sphere. But the churches were their training grounds.

A long history lies behind the charitable outreach. In colonial America the expectation immediately was that humanitarian instincts should be employed. Thus James Oglethorpe's Georgia colony may have been naïvely conceived and poorly executed. But its planners set forth an example of genuine concern for the imprisoned and poor of Europe, people who would cross the Atlantic to find better circumstances. Most colonies included people who made room for (fellow?) prisoners or poor, indentured servants who were aided to freedom by religious people. America immediately became a refugee center.

Not all the colonies made as much of their charitable purposes as did a few pace-setting ones. The human raw material that made up these colonies was as deficient as it always has been. People were out to advance themselves. But countless sermons and teaching situations were devoted to spreading motivation for Christian work for others. From the beginning, local churches and associations made provision for helping the sick and suffering. Hospitals were built, on primitive lines as they might have to be, but sophisticated in their intentions. Some colonies, notably those of William Penn and the Quakers, were seen to be pioneering ventures of service and love. Here and there in colonial America churches had already organized to spread relief among black slaves and freemen. While warfare came to complicate relations, efforts were made to help Indians in their bodily need. When relief for the poor was organized, this did not always or at first occur in secular and public orbits so much as through churches.

Colonial America was only a foretaste of what was to come later. At the time of the nation's birth a different set of religious premises inspired a new set of founding fathers. They might not talk about working for "the love of Christ" so much as in the pattern of "the life and morals of Jesus of Nazareth." But the people who gave life to the new nation, even when they were uneasy about Christian sectarianism and supernaturalism, were still sure that a just divine principle or providence in the universe would reward or punish people now or in another life for their moral outreach —and charity was one of the first spheres. From that point on churches had to justify their existence to the nonchurched by the scope and generosity of their humanitarian work.

The real explosion came early in the nineteenth century. While the Wesleyans were far from having a monopoly on the new spirit, they are representative embodiments of it. These followers of John Wesley or other evangelical and Methodist leaders took pains to show how Christian conversion was to produce works of holiness that could be measured in the face of human need. Another set of evangelical thinkers at this time developed with Samuel Hopkins the idea of "disinterested benevolence," in which one would seek Christ's way for the love of Christ and not out of quest for personal gain, including spiritual gain.

The result was what historian Charles Foster called an *Errand of Mercy,* one that was especially marked in England and America. The Marxian historian E. J. Hobsbawm says that in the period of expansion, Anglo-American evangelicalism was one of the few expanding religions. It was also expansive. People expected great things from God and attempted great things for him. They established societies for every kind of need (The New York Branch of the London Society for Providing Trusses for the Ruptured Poor), and supported them well. People of prominence in lay circles gave of their time and effort. Pioneering philanthropy was almost entirely an expression of Christian purposes and motives. People raised money, gave their time, inconvenienced themselves, undertook travel, held conventions and assemblies, paid visits, and in other ways went out of their way to face the human problems of their day. Their Marxian critics may say that they only papered over problems, or only corrected the bad aftermath of an industrial capitalist society they were reluctant to change or improve. There is some truth and sting to such charges. But overlooked in them is the genuineness of outreach on the part of millions who knew no other options and in whom the mixed bag of human motivation included true altruism and generosity.

While the spread of these lay, interchurch, largely independent agencies belonged chiefly to Protestants, they were by no means alone in humanitarianism. It is true that the modern movement of charity in evangelical circles is an event of world-historical importance. But it was not unique. As millions of Roman Catholics began to arrive, numerous orders of "sisters of mercy" under various names began to appear. Through them young women could sacrifice their lives and measures of their personal freedom in order to provide disciplined bases for helping others. Catholic charities paralleled those of Protestants. The Jewish humanitarian agencies have become proverbially successful in serving Jews, but there has also been a spillover, and much of the human relations and social work fraternity has a large Jewish contribution.

The motivations might change through the years. As government was assigned an ever larger role, the religious groups played a smaller part, if only proportionately. The growth of large corporations produced a generation of giants and barons, most of them religious, many of them eager to find a way to live with conscience and share their wealth. Today we might criticize the ethics of people whose way of life could put others out of business and who could destroy innocents through competition. But they came on the scene very suddenly, and it was hard for people to come to terms at once with the meaning of the new elite. Given those circumstances, it should at least be noted that they thought they did well as they built hospitals, seminaries, and agencies of charity, and their private correspondence and diaries show that very often they worked on the basis of religious views.

The graduated income tax cut into the proportionate size of such fortunes, and a developing welfare state took over many sectors of charitable expression. Religious groups have subsequently not always known how to act. Should they content themselves with efforts to plug the gaps and fill in the overlooked spaces? Should they provide different motives for doing what others around them who did not share their faith were doing? Whatever else these questions reveal, they show that Americans cannot lightly forget their heritage of sharing because of a faith they have known.

-10-

Theology Interpreting Experience

Americans have been a theologically inventive people. One can almost hear the suppressed chortles when such a claim is made. Certainly only a chauvinist or patriotic public relations expert would thus boast. European scholars might snicker at the very idea; they have been trained to see citizens of the United States as intense activists, often generous and pious people. But they almost never have to consult a work of theology produced by Americans; of that they are sure. By the standards with which they characteristically measure things, the people on the west side of the Atlantic have produced little that need concern them. They have been doers and not thinkers; when they have been thinkers, their thought has been derivative or superficial.

Reasons for such dismissals or even sniggering are

many, and they are understandable. Christianity in America has often appeared to be non- or even anti-intellectual. People in the New World have had their minds on so many things besides theological ideas, and life in their churches seems to have proceeded quite successfully, thank you, without the dubious contributions of thinkers who raise questions and who complicate life in general. Many of them might even pick up this page and either attack the assumption that theological inventiveness is a good thing or might at least shrug a "Who cares, anyhow?"

To make sense of these claims and attacks or dismissals we have to take some pains to say who cares or why anyone might. One way to do that will be to begin to define what is meant by theological inventiveness. Who should and does care? In a sense, most people do. When they ask important questions about where they came from and where they are going; why they are in a universe of apparent absurdity and meaninglessness or why they find meaning in it while others don't; how one can speak of a good God in a world of war and malignancy, people are opening the door for theological enterprise. Some of them may say that they simply have an experience of Zen or Yahweh or Jesus or karma and they resist interpretation. But experiences cannot be sustained all the time. Sooner or later they have to be made sense of, especially if they are to be shared by others. And whenever people use ideas and words to "make sense" of something in religion, they are doing on various levels what formal theologians have always done on their own.

To say that Americans have not always asked theological questions the way their ancestors did is not to say that they are not contributing to the tradition. Their ancestors also often changed their questions through the years. Thus in the Christian sphere, at one stage Christian theology had to do with how Christians could experience God as Father, Son, and Holy Spirit without worshiping three Gods. Out of such questions came the formulae about the divine Trinity. For other centuries they were preoccupied with questions about how the divine Son could also be the human Jesus of Nazareth, and "Christological controversies" resulted. Kings, bishops, emperors, all met to discuss historic theological questions and wars were fought over their definitions. Today the old issues remain alive but new ones have arisen also.

Some Americans have contended that since they believe only in a "simple gospel," they need do no thinking about it. They mistrust theologians for being complex, difficult, obscure, and prejudicial. They know enough history to know that religious intellectuals can confuse things as well as resolve them, and they know that loving God with the mind *only* has been the vice of some. Yet when the prophet Habakkuk asked the eternal "Why?" questions about the sufferings of the righteous, he was being theological. When Paul addressed Jews and Gentiles, both of whom had an experience of Jesus, he had to be theological when he tried to show them how to live together and to do so in a world of principalities and powers not of their own making.

Today's Jesus People, Pentecostals, charismatics,

Hasidic Jews, and Eastern religionists often come on as experiencers who need no theology or who despise it. But as they explicate their visions and revelations and move beyond a slogan or formula or two, they have to interpret life. The phrase "Jesus Saves" calls forth great theological endeavor: who is Jesus? From what and for what and by what means does he "save"?

Religious America has been full of communities of interpretation. Activist and experience-centered these may have been, but they have taken an uncommon amount of time in pulpits and classes or space in books and papers to set forth the meaning of action and experience. In this context a definition (though it is by no means the only appropriate one) for theology could be the interpretation of the life of a people in the light of a transcendent reference. That reference might be God the Father of Abraham, Isaac, Jacob, and of Jesus Christ; or it could be Providence, Progress, or Process as a "transcending" or "going beyond" reference point; but whenever people claim that something goes beyond the immediately visible and explainable part of their personal and social life, they verge on theology.

In America, plenty of theological ink has been spilled over Trinity and Christology, over the doctrines of the Virgin Mary and the survivals of Jewish mysticism. People have taken up historically conventional themes such as baptism, the Lord's Supper, atonement, reincarnation. But they have also stared out at a wilderness or hilltop and asked what was their errand. They have looked at the growing of America and asked what it meant to conceive of themselves as "the last, best hope of earth," as having a "manifest destiny" or mission. Why were they pushed into history and by what were they being pulled from it? What did it mean to be a nation "under God"? How should they relate to each other in the midst of pluralism; that is, how could they get along as a nation when that nation asked from them no specific commitment as to belief or nonbelief in God?

Responses to such questions appear on every hand. First, those who see no theological inventiveness in America have to reckon with the mere size and variety of the theological "cosa nostra" or establishment in America. Two hundred theological seminaries; scores of graduate schools of religion; hundreds if not thousands of departments of religion in colleges and universities; boards, bureaus, and staffs in denominations and ecumenical agencies; publication ventures all serve as reminders that not a few religious Americans subsidize and expect something, however indirect it may be, from men and women who are set aside professionally and vocationally to "do" theology. Seminarians pore over ancient texts and modern philosophies; conferees confer; task forces do their work. While the quality may not always be high, the enterprise is there.

Add to these the range of institutes at which people gather to take fresh looks at overlooked topics. Today they bring together the inquiry about religion in literature; they want to know the meaning of clinical experiences and the sciences of man; they need to know how to find religious outline and purpose in their social forms. Lay people gather to talk about God and vocations, business ethics, the spiritual meaning of modern medical problems, or life in the church. Sermons make theological efforts; few ministers merely repeat and shout biblical phrases (which are themselves often theological in the formal sense). They interpret the purposes of God in the life of nations, churches, persons.

Where churches and religious organizations are not attentive or capable, other agencies or people from different orbits of meaning take up the space theology once did. People like Erich Fromm, Margaret Mead, Erik Erikson, Saul Bellow, interpret life on quasi-theological lines. They may not always show how traditional views of God are to be related to contemporary life, but they will address that "God-shaped void" in people's lives and fill it somehow or other—with questions even if they cannot provide answers.

All these efforts have a long history. While the Western hemisphere has not produced many theological classics that belong in anthologies with the works of Augustine and Aquinas, Calvin and Schleiermacher, Maimonides or Karl Barth, different kinds of efforts merit attention. The story begins conventionally and appropriately in the New England colonies. From the early seventeenth century to the present a line of theological thought generated there has been studied. Sometimes historians and teachers have even treated it as "the only game in town" because it was the most respectable by European standards and the most influential all in all. A Catholic theologian may hear a setting forth of the thought of Jonathan Edwards and Horace Bushnell in the New England line and be impressed by it all, but may still feel he is in a foreign country. It has not always shaped his or her history. Today black theology, women's theology, and sect theology moves outside the old New England sphere. But the reaction should not lead to overreaction and the eventual overlooking of this heritage.

The New England fathers, as scholar Perry Miller and others have shown, not only came across the Atlantic burdened with theological questions. They brought along formidable theological systems, or produced their own. Many of the early leaders had been well-trained Puritans who used the logic of their day to expound Scriptures and the thought of the English Reformation. At one time all their efforts were dismissed as being bizarrely beside the point. They did not seem to be talking about a real world. They were too sure about divine purpose, especially for people who believed his will was somehow inscrutable.

More recently their thought has been extensively rediscovered and reappraised. They were talking about a real world, about life in covenanted communities, about God's purposes in New England. They came with a kind of script in hand; the Bible outlined their exodus and their exile. They were on an errand into the wilderness. Theirs was a city set upon a hill, but they did not think the story was finished. They were here to complete the Reformation or to help prepare for a coming kingdom. No random events marked colonial life;

if the skies darkened or the children turned wayward, someone must ask about what went wrong. Someone must repent and find a new way.

The early diaries, legislative codes, and popular expressions were as theological as the sermons. In Jonathan Edwards many have seen the coming together of the two. He was attentive to common people's religious experiences just as he was sure that God has something to say to the people of his town, colony, and hemisphere. But Edwards was not alone in New England, and New England was not alone. The pious Henry Melchior Muhlenburg, who knew *ecclesia plantanda,* the church must be planted, had to ask about what church was in the Pennsylvania wilderness beyond Philadelphia. The Quakers were sure that the divine light would break through their holy commonwealth.

The semisecular national founding fathers were discontented with and opposed to much of the Calvinism or Trinitarianism theology in the churches. But they did not stop talking about God and providence, meaning and mission. They translated it to other terms. One historian, Carl Becker, spoke of *The Heavenly City of the Eighteenth Century Philosophers.* He knew what he was doing because he knew what they were doing; they took the shell and outline of the old religious systems and supplied their own. Theirs remains a part of American public school religion, the faith of Boy Scouts and service clubs, of people who never enter churches. They make much of equality, justice, and freedom as being somehow divinely assured and rich in new meanings.

The nineteenth century saw a flowering of these and other lines of thought. Roman Catholics arrived in significant numbers. They had to leave behind their libraries and seminaries; they were often dependent and derivative; they often seemed too busy to think. Probably not until the 1950s did they produce American thinkers who could hold their own with European scholars. But in the rough and tumble of immigrant and frontier life, less highly lettered people like the maverick Orestes Brownson or the journalist-educator-priest Father Isaac Hecker showed what it meant to discern the meaning of Catholic experience in America.

Continental Protestants arrived with a great deal of theological baggage. If some churches despised intellectuality, Philip Schaff the church historian argued, they owed it to themselves to take a look at what the Pennsylvania Lutherans or the Reformed at his Mercersburg seminary were discussing. The New England theology unfolded at Harvard and Andover and Yale, or in the pulpits of Hartford, in the work of Nathaniel William Taylor or Horace Bushnell. In Boston the liberal Unitarians argued their case through William Ellery Channing's writings, or more radically through Theodore Parker's. If these churchly names do not mean too much to persons today, most people know that Ralph Waldo Emerson and the transcendentalists produced new formulae that would replace Christian ones. They talked about Over-soul and absolute spirit. William James studied the *Varieties of Religious Experience* in psychological terms and with Emerson and

Edwards—as historian William A. Clebsch has shown —tried to help Americans become "at home" in the universe.

American Jews like all Jews may not historically have used the term theology at all, but for centuries they have been theologians in these terms and may have produced the model for what Americans have done: interpreted divine purpose in the light of a transcendent reference. It is in the public sphere where much theologizing has gone on. For some, Abraham Lincoln is the center of the endeavor. He spoke of the "last, best hope of earth" but was sure that God would judge it. He looked at warring sides and asked them not to claim that God was on their own. But he asked partisans to try to conform to God's own will, mysterious as it may be. Many people have helped generate what Walter Lippmann called "a public philosophy" and have done so by reference to God and transcendent meanings. Theirs is an unfinished work in an ever-unfolding drama. Americans have not "not thought" but they have thought in different but evidently appropriate ways about their life and purpose.

-11-

The Creativity of Ethics and Morals

WHEN PEOPLE want to say something derogatory about American religion, they attack it for its moralism. They say it has been too Puritan. This means, in the eyes of the attackers, that the quest for the moral life has been too grim and too repressive. There is no tolerance of human frailty and no enjoyment of human frivolity. Everything in life has to be measured by whether or not someone is doing good and is not having a good time. On the other hand, when people want to compliment citizens of the United States for their spirituality, they usually say that they have been ethical and moral. They at least make a contribution to doing good.

Significantly, it is far more rare for them to attack religion here for being too stupid or mindless or to compliment it for achievements of the mind. It is rare for spiritual forces to be criticized for their shoddy art and expression, or to be lauded for their great achievements in the fields of architecture or poetry. The debate revolves around the matter of being good and being bad, doing well and doing evil. Ethics and morality is at stake.

Why? Why measure and divide things along this line? Any self-respecting American knows why: ethics is what religion is all about. It asks for nobility of character, proper respect for the difference between right and wrong, and the production of a way of life that allows for expression of the good. It might surprise one to learn that such an evaluation is late and rare in religious history.

Most of the time religions have been measured by how satisfactorily they explain human existence through their rites and sacrifices. How much meaning do they give to the seasons and the rhythms of the year? How well do their initiation rites prepare warriors for battle? How well do their cave paintings and dances cast magical spells over animals so that the hunt will be successful? Are the huts in a village properly lined up so that they reflect the way the universe is put together? Will rain come after a chant? Can disease be done away with by the witch doctor? May I be "in tune with the universe"?

In the Western world biblical religion introduces a note of ethical concern that is distinctive though not unique in religion. Other faiths have not been unconcerned with good and bad in moral life—they simply have not made it so central. Let it also be said that not all biblical religion produces moralism. The consistent biblical note of grace, the reference to God's initiating activity, should minimize moral grimness for Christians. The Hebrew Scriptures and later Jewish writings also balance their ethical seriousness with everything from an erotic Song of Songs to injunctions to "taste and see that the Lord is good" or to "be still and know" that he is God.

In the modern world, however, ethics came to be the measurement, especially in a free society such as the one developed in America two centuries ago. If there are to be "satisfied customers," they will have to be convinced that religion produces good. Thus in the United States religious organizations in the past have tended to be tax-exempt. The exemptions are not defended because churches' stained-glass windows are so beautiful that the society cannot do without them. Nor are they defended because synagogue chant is necessary for life in a free society. No, the defense comes because religious groups are seen as moral agencies, contributing to the good of the community.

Justification for chaplaincies in the military usually have to do with the moral guidance, counsel, and example these bring. The nation is tolerant of the theological eccentricities that go with these various ministries to the military. But it is most appreciative of the ethical contribution. When a real estate developer advertises churches in a new town he is, of course, trying to sell houses to people who want to go to church. But he will also describe his community as being capable of more likely forms of moral stability as a result of the religious institutions.

The most familiar charges against church people

have to do with ethical lapses. They are a "bunch of hypocrites" when they pray and are pious but still gouge and cheat. They are a corrupt establishment when they say the right things but support the evil structures of life. The contemporary scene allows numerous angles of vision on these realities.

Thus religion is tied with personal morality through the cycles of life. Sunday school and parochial schools are looked on with favor by the larger society not because they teach the peculiarities of each faith but because they form the ethical value systems of a new generation. Strange stories about ancient monarchs and miracle workers are tolerated by adults who do not believe them because they generate morality. The home is peculiarly regarded as a place where religious virtues will produce good adults. When something goes wrong with the nation's moral fabric, something in the churches' permissiveness can be blamed: this is a high compliment to the ethical productivity of the good home.

As young people grow, the nation expends much energy and hope inculcating moral patterns, often on a religious base. The Boy Scouts and the Girl Scouts have their counterparts in dozens of religious organizations; the YMCA and YWCA were founded to provide moral homes away from home for slightly older young people. Congregations cast around for young ministers who will have the ears of the youth, again with their moral development in mind.

While churches for the adult world keep many evidences that they are not only grimly productive of good works (whenever they merely celebrate the works of God in art, music, dance, liturgy, prayer, or when they produce social events), when Americans really turn serious they support churches as moral agencies. And these customers must be satisfied, because through the years an impressive number of Americans have made sacrifices for them. And from these churches have issued people whom their critics dismiss as do-gooders but whom many of their beneficiaries regard as saints. They have helped sensitize Americans to the needs and circumstances of remote peoples in other lands or in poverty pockets in their own.

Social ethics is a popular field of study, however controversial it may be. In this area, people probe the effects religious institutions have on people in groups, or they ask how the social structures permit moral concerns to be embodied or how they frustrate them. When the people who use social scientific approaches interview or take polls of Americans they like to ask about the part religion plays. They regularly turn up worries about the state of religion. People usually believe that religion should shape morality, and that it did so with more telling effect in the past.

Moral achievement has been impressive. When one looks at the lay and clerical leaders who have risked their material goods and reputations for the sake of ethical concerns, there is little that should lead people to be ashamed. In the recent past, as we note elsewhere in this book, much of the movement for racial concord came from high-risk people in the religious world. For whatever excesses may have appeared, during the Vietnamese war's earlier stages it was a coalition that included religious leaders that successfully kept the moral question of American policy on the people's minds. In Arab-Israeli encounters, both sides make moral appeals to American religionists. The case for civil liberties, while it is sometimes opposed by religious people of censorious or repressive bent, has also been supported by men and women who regard the broadest expression of freedom to be congruent with their faith.

The various churches often support lobbies in Washington, D.C., to represent their ethical positions on matters that concern them. Sometimes these have to do with legislation concerning alcoholic beverages or drugs or gambling; just as often they have less to do with personal vice and more to do with public virtue. They seek legislation that would improve the chances for justice, prosperity, and peace. These cannot always be popular. They inconvenience people and challenge prejudices; they may sometimes be expressed by self-righteous and self-assured people. But they do keep alive moral debate.

The modes of moral discourse are many. For hundreds of years Americans have welcomed sermons that cajole listeners into moral patterns. Probably more effective have been the classes and discussion groups where people have been free to take on a difficult question in the light of a revelation or tradition. What does our Scripture tell us to do about peace, about working toward open housing? Anything? What does it say to us when we are divided over the matter? In addition to sermons and classes, support of the various boards and bureaus through whom people in the modern world make impacts is another illustration of ethical concern. And most effective religious people form their own cells and units for direct action to help them face up to injustices and to implement moral patterns.

The heroes in American religious life are and have been largely moral heroes, people who undertook risks in order to live out what their conscience called them to. Those who had big enough enemies eventually came to be known as saints.

A long tradition lies behind these contemporary expressions. While plenty of slugabeds and good-for-nothings stocked the ships that made their way across to colonial America, few of us look back on our flawed forefathers without noting the nobility of purpose so many of them expressed. Some of them had no place to go but America. But more of them chose to come because they were not free to pursue their ideals and patterns on other shores. They wanted to put an order into their lives. Their pages are almost drearily filled with concern about how they can provide a moral laboratory for their children on the American shores.

Centuries later some of their efforts are derided or criticized for having been overly harsh. But after deductions have been made for the humorlessness and harshness, it is hard not to admire people who cared so much about serving God and being good to others. When there was a shortage of nails and the enterprising hardware man Robert Keayne raised the price—as any good capitalist would in the face of a shortage—the good town fathers and elders asked what effect this would have on the community as a whole. Mr. Keayne was disciplined and chastised for this act and had to make an "apologia" to the gathered congregation of townspeople. The records of town after town show that nothing was taken for granted, that every detail of life had to be addressed from a moral point of view.

If the Franklins and Jeffersons wanted to break free from the more dogmatic and sterile aspects of these heritages, they did not stop being moral and even moralist. Benjamin Franklin was not interested in dogma. He was supportive of churches not for what they held separately in belief but for what they contributed in common to the good living. He may have been a rakish old soul on the sly and may have had a way with the women, but he was also scrupulous as he helped a society turn from Puritan to Yankee moralism. Thomas Jefferson may have had little room for theological speculation and his worship seemed routine. But he spent White House evenings snipping out the non-supernatural elements of the Gospels and putting together *The Life and Morals of Jesus of Nazareth* out of the remains. Others honored at bicentennial time are equally remembered for seeking to inculcate moral norms and patterns into America's public life.

When people not of these lineages came to the American shores, they were often scored for not living up to every detail of the old codes. Thus Roman Catholics and continental Protestants were accused of promoting "the continental Sabbath" as a time of gaiety when they should have been sombre and reflective. But these immigrants were not immoralists just because they were different. Many of the Catholics were taught by Jansenist priests, men who have been dubbed "Catholic Calvinist moralists." And the less severe still made strong demands on Catholics, who have been as impressive as their co-religionists in stressing the need for good living. Jewish humor is sometimes bitter about the high moral expectations of synagogue and home, but that humor often barely disguises a high regard for a way of life that taught people how to employ religion for the care of others.

When a historian like Timothy Smith looks back on *Revivalism and Social Reform* he sees in the middle of nineteenth-century American evangelicalism not only people having whooping good emotional binges in camp meetings or ecstatic jags and jerks in revivals. He sees earnest and loving people setting out also on a social gospel path.

Their voluntary societies were not devoted always and only to spreading tracts and Sunday schools and missionaries, nor to imposing their high standards on people who could not comprehend them, though they did all this, too. They were just as concerned to make honest efforts at discerning the true physical and social needs of their contemporaries and then finding religious grounds and humane means for addressing them. Some of their efforts may have been misguided and may have issued in legislation of ambiguous effect, as in the case of Prohibition or the prohibition of birth control. But in the context of the possibilities of their day they did what they could to produce a better nation.

The Social Gospel movement is sometimes looked back on and faulted for a superficially optimistic theology and even for transforming some classic Christian teachings beyond recognition. Sometimes it was in the hands of people who would not get their own hands dirty. But it was also a quite original expression of American Christians who wanted to find ways to "bring in the kingdom" as they would put it, or "Christianize the social order," in the emerging industrial-urban world. Modern Catholicism has generated ethical endeavors in the field of labor relations and industrial change of equal potency.

Today's counter-cultural religious movements may try to bring a balancing gaiety and frivolity to religion. But they are not likely to cause Americans to expect less in the way of moral good from the religious forces whose "customers" they have become.

-12-

The Opportunity for Prophecy

JOSEPH PULITZER once told journalists that the task of the newspaper was to "afflict the comfortable and to comfort the afflicted." Some have properly seen in this little phrase a summary of fulfilled religion, especially of biblical faith. The Bible assumes that not all is right with the world or with the humans in it. They are to come to wholeness. If they are comfortable and proud it is likely that they will miss the deeper stirrings of the spirit and will separate themselves from the claims of God and the condition of other mortals. On the other hand, God destines them for a whole life, and does not reveal himself as enjoying their suffering or despair. Therefore in their affliction they have a right to and a need for comfort.

How to keep the two in balance or tension has always been a difficult art. In history it has so often happened that the comfortable attract preachers who will cater to their interest and dispense more comfort, as if pouring more syrup on a full pitcher of syrup is of help to anyone. And just as frequently the oppressed of the world are confronted by people who misuse religion to drive them deeper from the sources of hope. American religion has seen both these evidences in rich supply.

The two halves of religion could be called the integrative and the disruptive. When people are "out of joint" with the universe, God, and themselves, they experience salvation when they are integrated into a circle of acceptant people and find meaning in a message of acceptance such as the Christian gospel imparts. But very often no sooner are they thus integrated than they overstate or overexperience the case and lose their touch with the source of their worth and value. They think they have produced their own health. Then the message of God is to come to them and disrupt their circle and their way. He has to cause new ferment and pain, just as the surgeon does when he probes a sensitive spot in the body of a person who does not want to acknowledge illness.

The relation between afflicting the comfortable and comforting the afflicted is spelled out in many different ways in the Scriptures. People are pictured as being lost and lonely. They do not know themselves or their families, human or divine community. They are lost in a wilderness and find no purpose in life. Then the prophet will say, "Call a solemn assembly. Sanctify a fast." In other words, set up a sanctuary and gather people for divine worship. There God's gracious gifts will be dispensed. The afflicted are thus comforted.

Biblical faith knows just as much the dangers of

such gatherings and comforts. Almost always the chosen people think they merited chosenness. They become prideful and complacent. Whereupon the prophet comes on the scene and says, speaking for Yahweh, "I despise the noise of your solemn assemblies." Get out of the sanctuary and away from self-justifying religion. Be with the poor and the despairing. Change your way of life.

This tradition is picked up in the New Testament, for example, in the career of John the Baptist. The people come to this prophet and he gets their attention by afflicting the comfortable: he calls them a generation of vipers and advises them that the axe is laid at the root of the trees. Yet he also comforts the afflicted by the announcement of the coming one who in the face of their repentance will usher in a new age and the kingdom of God itself. Jesus no less than John knew how to do both. He never fulfilled his ministry in the face of a group—whether it be his disciples or individuals or larger more diffuse groups—without discerning their dual needs and ministering to them.

The disruptive, discomforting, or prophetic side of ministry Paul Tillich called "the protestant principle." He did not simply identify this with Protestant churches. Instead he saw it as a principle whereby people never confuse their ways with God's, and wherein they permit God to judge not their neighbors or bad causes but their own good causes.

The prophetic principle is not really a personality issue, though some people of sour and dour temperament have gravitated to the prophetic role for the wrong reasons: they simply never liked anything they ever saw. In the better instances, the prophet is one who, for the sake of a better future, takes images from the past and projects them on a screen ahead of the people. He then asks these people to change their ways to live into these images. Thus God can work on them and among them. On those terms a prophet is not prideful or "prophetistic"; he can be loving as was the prophet Hosea who suffered with the people rather than railed at them.

The prophetic note has been repeatedly present in American religion and remains with us today. It is visible in the humblest of circumstances, wherever even the simple people who would be embarrassed to be thought of as prophets or spokesmen for God try to run things for him. Instead, they inconvenience themselves by quiet witness to his purpose. Often they can insinuate their way into a congregation's or a community's consciousness by the way they live rather than by what they say. Lives are rearranged as a consequence. There is nothing peculiar about the fact that this happens in America, but it is noteworthy that the prophetic witness did not disappear in the pluralistic jumble of American life.

The American environment has encouraged the development of strong local congregations. Among them the temptation has been especially strong to encourage prejudice among the like-minded. Therefore it is all the more impressive that in such congregations the prophetic word has survived. During the civil rights struggles of the sixties many a prominent professor, bureaucrat, author, or journalist would be called a prophet for demonstrating for racial change in the American south or in a northern city. This is not the place to criticize such efforts; the believer is called to witness out of conviction in many kinds of circumstances. Often personal courage of a sort was called for, as anyone who stared the forces of law and order in the eye in Selma or Cicero could readily testify. But in many cases the term prophet was misapplied, because the communal risks were small. People would simply honor the demonstrator or spokesman more.

When a local minister or lay leader would engage in similar activities, however, more risk and thus more power was involved. He would have to explain to the congregation what were the conscience reasons and the mandates from the word of God that impelled such activity. The reasons may not always have been compelling, but they carried a note of special weight and worth because these leaders were so identified in bonds of love with people to whom they wanted to keep on being responsible. It would be hard to record the countless times in the American past and present when a local leader mounts a pulpit or rostrum and says effectively, "Thou art the man!" (or woman).

Not all prophets grow up in such quiet circumstances, and the American scene has regularly recognized people who by their charisma and their risks successfully project better futures and promote inconveniencing ways to arrive there. Our times do not lack people who seek justice or peace on such terms. Most of them are not unfamiliar with the interiors of jails because they are at home with the interior of the Christian message. The word of Jesus, "Woe to you when all men speak well of you!" is not likely to be applied to true prophets.

The prophetic motif is built into a basic interpretation of American religious thought. In the recent past it has been exemplified by Reinhold Niebuhr, for example. The mid-century prophet fused two of the best streams in American religion. On one hand, he cared about the nation and its political and social processes. He could never be accused of not being involved with its life, whether as a pastor in industrial Detroit, a teacher at a seminary, or an advisor to the mighty of his day in New York and national government. Such a locale has caused many before and after him to mute their criticism in order to gain and retain a hearing from the mighty.

Niebuhr, however, used "the protestant principle of prophetic protest" whenever such temptations came along. Over against a comfortable and prideful nation he would then thunder or remark in quiet irony with the psalmist that "he who sitteth in the heavens shall laugh" at such comfort and pretense. Over against his own community of Protestant churches he could be more critical than he ever cared to be toward others. Martin Luther King also repeatedly demonstrated his love for the nation for which he "had a dream." But on biblical grounds he also scored its violence and hatreds until he became a victim of both. In the modern world we are close enough to such figures to know their flaws; that is just as well. The old-time prophets had them, too. These remind us that they are men and women and not gods, and that God works through the flawed, according to Christian testimony.

Similarly Abraham Joshua Heschel showed both sides of religion. He taught Jews and other Americans to hallow and honor all of life, to affirm God and enjoy the *Seder*. But when he thought that this good nation was unjust and murderous in Vietnam he led protests against military and political party, at considerable personal risk.

The latter-day prophets have former-day precedents, and any fair assessment of American religion has to recognize these antecedents. From the first there were those who were critical of others who despoiled the virgin wilderness and misused the people who already inhabited it. Such words from Quaker spokesmen or New England and Virginian ministers were not popular, especially when little wars broke out or massacres ensued. It was not popular for people almost from the beginning to protest the timeless practice of enslaving people for economic purpose, but America's believers produced such protesters.

The New England tradition here as so often shows both elements. But afflicting the comfortable was almost a normal activity among the old divines. A generation brought up on the bad choice in their textbooks of Jonathan Edwards' grouchy and threatening sermon on "Sinners in the Hands of an Angry God" may have difficulty comprehending that he was in love with his people and their environment. But as lavish as he was in enjoying God's surprising conversions among them, he was also disconcerted to see their neglectfulness and complacency. Then he could thunder. The religious Great Awakening is remembered as a time of heartwarming religion, but it constantly embodied afflicters of the comfortable.

The prophetic note was not as prominent among the people who, somewhat apart from the biblical prophetic tradition, helped spiritually to inspire a new nation. The advocates of "republican religion," the kind of new national faith, are often dismissed as optimistic and benevolent congratulators of their own contemporaries. But when people did not live up to the blessings of liberty they could scold. Thomas Jefferson also had what one historian called a "darker side." It was reflected in his fears that the new republic could not long endure and that a revolution might be needed every few years for the purity of the nation.

This line was carried on in the nineteenth century by historians. David Noble has called their work "Jeremiads." George Bancrofts and his contemporaries had a picture of what the future America should be. It should keep its covenant with nature and simplicity. Yet his contemporaries constantly were wavering, and they needed to have judgment pronounced on what they were corrupting.

The advocates of new religion, the transcendentalists, sometimes look like "positive thinkers" about a universe at home with itself. But they also produced what might be called a "protestantism outside Protestantism." The more consistent among them, like Henry David Thoreau, were so preoccupied with the vision of a coming society of nonviolence that they would suffer jail or ignominy for their principles. The abolitionists often had to move beyond the confines of church religion in order to keep alive a note they took from biblical prophecy. If foreign visitors found the ministers too timid, too ready to draw a too narrow circle around the sphere in which they would judge people, someone else regularly rose to do the judging.

The little Utopian communities that dotted the nineteenth-century landscape were often filled with optimistic and usually cheerful people. But the very arrangements of their communities were themselves judgments on the grasping and overly busy competitivenesses of their contemporaries. Throughout the century despite great personal hazard American black freemen would effectively speak quiet words of prophecy to their white contemporaries. And in noisier fashion, leaders of slave revolts would garb their criticisms in biblical terms to seek a promised land for their people. The slavery issue aside—and that is a huge "aside"—the evangelicals constantly called into question many features of life around them.

Later comers, such as the large numbers of immigrant Roman Catholics, Jews, and Eastern Orthodox, were not as free as the earlier arrivals to engage in open criticism of the society and the people in it. They were busy helping their people catch up, establish themselves, and adapt in it. They did not dare risk all. They were honestly appreciative of life in the new world as opposed to that in the old. So their criticism was often muted. Yet when occasion demanded they would minister to their people and the larger society by calling into question the compromises and complacencies that afflicted both.

The Social Gospel can be seen in this context as a prophetic movement. Its spokesmen like Walter Rauschenbusch regularly reread the biblical prophets, the medieval sectarians, the leaders of the left-wing or radical Reformation, and applied their results to the world of their contemporaries. They were more successful at condemning evil in social structures than in individuals, but plenty of other people were taking care of individual problems and needs. In the midst of the self-satisfied progressivisms of the early twentieth century these people reintroduced futurist language and present inconvenience.

In the middle of the twentieth century the Niebuhr prophets spoke of their movement as "Christian realism." At bicentennial time numbers of evangelicals have expressed discontent with evangelical social complacency and are writing their own new chapter in the unfinished history of American judgment and self-judgment.

Epilogue: Turning Pro to Con

No ONE can read reflections on two centuries of religion in national life without developing a deep appreciation of self-sacrificing men and women of vision who left a legacy of service to others and witness to truth. The reasons for feeling positive about what is inheritable after two centuries are impressive. While we have not consistently focused on specifically Christian responses, the Christian majority in America can certainly feel at home with many of the basic results of the national spiritual life and endeavor. Numbers of biblical words urge the people of God to be supportive of their surrounding civil society, to help men and women of good will care for the earth, for community, for persons.

And yet, there is a disturbing note that has to go along with the appreciations. The biblical word is never content to let people rest with the status quo. The prophets are aware of the strong temptations people have to make idols of their productions, their tribes, their circumstances. Normally the word of God is to come first as a disruptive word, one that shows the distance between the Kingdom of God or the wonders of his creative and redeeming acts and everything human. That note dare not be muted permanently in American life.

From some points of view, it is urgent that we begin to raise questions that might turn *Pro* into *Con* in our observations of American religiosity. This is not because we cannot let well enough alone, or have crabby personalities, or are filled with our own spiritual pride over against the achievements of others. There can always and only be two motives in such second looks. The first has to grow out of the religious vision that asks us to measure human efforts in the light of the word of God. The other is the view of human need that inspires better efforts.

In these terms we are left with questions, one that grows out of each topic.

Has America made what it might of its spiritual achievements? Have the church-goers been truly liberated and liberating people? Have they developed whole and open personalities? More often than not they seem to be able to divert their attention from what might enhance the human spirit and toward what might lead to their material gain.

Is the American's historical sense used chiefly to help give people a sense of identity and worth? Or is it not just as frequently employed to build up a sense of the pride over nation? American memories conveniently forget whatever is embarrassing; they dwell on that which justifies themselves in their own eyes.

140

The question has to be raised as to whether the pious communities of America have not huddled together so much that they cannot hear even true words that come from outside their circles. Is it not true that a price has been paid for the chumminess born of the sense of belonging? Those who do not belong to the right circle may not always be despised, but they often are neglected.

Americans make much of their cosmopolitan and missionary spirit. Without question, it has often served them and other people well. But on balance, can we take satisfaction from the outreach if this has meant using other people to our own ends—whether imperially, economically, or culturally? Have they been appreciated for their own sakes?

Tolerance can be a virtue. But in the style of the comic strip character Charlie Brown, it can also be a mark of indifferentism and the inability to see when a stand has to be taken. Is America guilty of this superficial tolerance and, concurrently, of seeing all tolerance fade when it is tested by people who really stand at some distance from the approved values?

Yes, America has welcomed various peoples. Some of them came as slaves against their will. Others came against their own preference, because there was nowhere else to go. Still others came as adventurers and profiteers. Have many of them ever learned to get along with each other, or do we not even today need other races and peoples to serve as a floor for our own self-esteem?

Visitors marvel at the participation of American lay

people in religion. They ask just as often whether some of this participation does not have to do more with selfish ego-satisfaction than it does with serving God for his own sake. And has some of it appeared in part because religious leadership has been so vapid?

Women "never had it so good" and "have come a long way" in American life. But churches are supposed to be in God's advance guard of liberation. Why have so many changes for the better in the status of women had to come independently of and often even in competition with the practices and professions of ruling males in the churches?

The two centuries in America have been marked by generous humanitarian outpourings, and religious forces have often set the pace. Are there trends now, in the day of a semi-welfare state, whereby religious people are losing their impetus and skill, their vision of human need? Are they depersonalizing their works of love and turning them over to remote bureaucracies?

We can be glad that so many people who lacked leisure and resources of great research libraries reflected as often as they did about the ways of God to man. Can we be proud of the anti-intellectualism that most visitors associate with American religionists? Why is it sometimes seen as a denial to "love the Lord thy God with all thy mind" while the heart and soul get all the credit?

Without question the religious groups in the American past and present have given a high priority to those who would try to show that their faith is active in love, to produce the good works that follow from the gifts of grace. But is it not also true that sometimes the efforts to do good are paraded before God and man as reasons for pride; and is it not equally true that for many believers, little energy goes 'nto asking how religious people should act in the world, especially when such action inconveniences them?

Religious freedom and the surprising mixture of people with differing viewpoints made America a staging ground for prophets and nuts, misfits and eccentrics. All kinds of people have their say, and they often say something critical. But it is also necessary to ask why so little of the criticism has come from religious norms, and why we have found so many ways to neglect or counter the little bit that trickles past all the self-defensive screens the citizens set up to see that their life is not disturbed.

The questions remain to plague, to nag, to inspire. Those who feel that the national bicentennial years can turn positive appreciation into idolatry of nation and self can also serve by asking another set of questions. One recommendation for those who would be ready to pursue this course would be: flip the book over, and start from the other side.

During the past seventeen years Martin E. Marty has published seventeen books. He has written articles for countless journals and newspapers, and has contributed to or edited numerous books while contributing to the major encyclopedias.

Dr. Marty is a Lutheran minister who served in the pastorate for ten years before becoming Professor of the History of Modern Christianity at the University of Chicago, where he also had earned his Ph.D. degree. There he teaches in the Divinity School, the Committee on the History of Culture, and is an associate in the History Department.

He is associate editor of the weekly *The Christian Century* and editor of the biweekly newsletter *Context*. With four sons and a foster son (Joel, John, Peter, James, and Micah), Dr. and Mrs. Marty live in Riverside, Illinois. They also have a place on an island where during the summers, far from telephones and electricity, Dr. Marty writes his books —including this one.

The island represents the more leisurely side of a busy life; in addition to his teaching, lecturing, and writing, the author also finds time for family, friends, and numerous avocational interests.

Martin E. Marty

The Pro & Con Book of Religious America

A Bicentennial Argument

Martin E. Marty

The Pro & Con Book of Religious America

A Bicentennial Argument

Word Books, Publisher
Waco, Texas

To
John H. Tietjen

In the face of "con" religion, a witness

Contents

Preface

THIS BOOK tries to tell in brief outline what is wrong
—religiously and spiritually—with the two-hundred-
year-old United States. The reader who feels it is one-
sided need merely flip it over to read the other side
since the second half of the book tells what is right
about the same nation. Each chapter has a counterpart. This format is designed to stimulate creative
debate within and among persons during the years surrounding the bicentennial observance—though I hope
it will be useful for many years to come since it deals
with what may be among the most important issues
with which America has to wrestle.

The two halves of the book can each be read in a sitting or two. However, the reader may wish to intersperse chapters from one half with those that are their
counterparts in the other half. Or the twelve themes
can be taken up by discussion groups, congregations,
or classes, through twelve months. The chapters are
kept brief for this purpose. They are exactly what
they claim to be: arguments. They are not anecdotally
crammed. They are not allegories or epic narratives.
They are succinct and economical, designed to inspire
readers, singly or in groups, to fill in the details out of
their own experience, observation, or reading.

Each chapter begins with several paragraphs outlining the spiritual, national, or personal value of the
theme. Then readers are invited to look around them,

to seek signs or confirmations of that theme and argument in the contemporary world that is in range of their vision, to think about that reality in a special way. Finally, each chapter has several pages on main themes or events from the past. These usually deal with colonial, revolutionary, nineteenth century, or contemporary historical motifs. The proportions of the chapter are shaped so that both those who have interest and competence in history and those who do not (or think they do not) will find themselves addressed. Because the American spirit has been shaped more by biblical faith, Jewish and especially Christian, it has been most frequently assumed or elaborated upon, though some attention has also been devoted to other varieties of religion.

Why such a book? The author has reason to have four worries about readers' responses. They might ask: Is it all a game, arranged for point-scorers in debating societies? If the author sees both sides, is he for a kind of middling and even wishy-washy course between the extremes? Can he really mean what he says in both PRO and CON halves, or are his fingers crossed, and is he tongue-in-cheek? Can he be thoughtful; has he thought things through and is his mind clear?

The readers or users will judge, but they are not likely to resent my stating the case. Think of the arrangement as a game, if by this is meant that the experience of struggling with such themes can be creative and pleasurable. But its goal is not for debating points in contests so much as for helping people make up their minds about decisive issues. Almost never does it set-

tle for compromises. Instead, I believe that if people can live with contradiction and paradox, they will learn more from the extremes of national life than from carefully balanced and compromised paragraphs. Third, does he mean it? Yes. I believe that I can back up and richly document the assertions in both halves, and I know that I believe everything I have written about each—and yet have seldom been accused of having a divided mind or being schizoid. American history itself is full of extremes, of paradox, contradiction, and complexity. The ability to live with that history can be health-giving. Finally, I hope that I am thoughtful. The book distills and condenses elements of a career-long concern for American religious history and the spiritual dimensions of today's culture. In such a short book one cannot say everything that should be said about these concerns, but what is said can represent the larger story.

At bicentennial time reflective people can look around them in the present and also backward toward the past in order to move responsibly into the early decades of the nation's third century. This book argues that theme and samples twelve illustrative subthemes.

—MARTIN E. MARTY
Chicago, Illinois

Part I
The American Spirit

1. A Materialistic Society
   versus A Spiritual Society
2. Amnesia and Present-Mindedness
   versus Historical Awareness
3. The Lonely Individualist
   versus The Spirit of Community
4. Provincialism and Nationalism
   versus An International Ethos

-1-

A Materialistic Society

IF EVER a nation was free to be worldly, it was America. The Bible warns against "loving the things of this world," but America has been so full of things to love that it is no wonder its citizens have fallen into temptation and loved them. Foreign visitors have always been stunned at the materialism of the people. Commerce dominates all that they do. Banks, not churches, have been the characteristic buildings. The hills and fields are full of resources, and the people plunder them.

If some nations in the past took steps to check the worldliness that tempted them, this was not the case with the United States. Most earlier societies saw to it that some sort of spiritual purpose was written into their founding or ruling documents and laws. Some commitment to God was made in their covenants, the terms of agreement for their life together. Not so with the United States. Its Constitution does not ask

the people to pay heed to sacred things in any way; at best it tries to see that the government does not get involved one way or another. The Supreme Court has called this a policy of "wholesome neutrality." Few would want to change that policy. But it tells us much about the ground rules of national life, so we can watch the game as it has been played.

The indictment can be simple and direct. Whoever observes the nation in action quickly comes to the conclusion that people most of the time arrange their lives the same way whether God exists or not. While few openly oppose religion, most of them serenely ignore the claims of God on their lives. The visitor cannot see a higher standard of morality or sympathy in America than he or she would find in a nonChristian society or one which is advertised as being less religious. Each year the distractions grow. People extend their weekends and remove themselves from their houses of worship. They build high-rise apartments and climb into them, never to emerge on a Sabbath, unless for a day at the beach. Were someone to bring a spiritual point of view to business life, he would either be done in by the competition or sent off to a mental clinic. Business people are supposed to compete at the expense of others.

Mass media of communication almost never use their prime time to divert listeners, viewers, or readers from their earthbound visions. Politicians may give lip service to the name of God at the beginning or end of their speeches or their day's work, but their grasp of what God wants of them does not often show

up in their policies. The editors of a national magazine once asked, "Is the world put together the way our magazine is?" Many magazines have sections devoted to the world of politics, business, the arts, religion, athletics, and entertainment. Religion is boxed into a section; people can take it or leave it. Most people know something about the worlds of sports or diversions. They know almost nothing of the people or events that call them to deeper, more spiritual concerns. The pocketbook is another clue: bills for liquor or entertainment are far higher than are items budgeted for uplift, inspiration, or service.

These signs, open to anyone's eye, are only beginnings. They have to do with external behavior. It is important for people in the 1970s to determine what lies behind these patterns. It may be asked, "Why should we have to face up to our worldliness, our materialism, and our selfishness?" Several answers come to mind. First, at the bicentennial we stand the best chance in years of taking time to define ourselves, to try to tell stories that are true. Pure religion demands accurate stories. There should be no illusions. We dare not call ourselves one thing and be another. We have to know how our lives are arranged.

Second, such a story will help a new generation make decisions about life. If we wish to follow religious visions, we have to know something about the odds, the distractions, the opposition. Finally, people who stand in the line of biblical religion know that they are not to delude themselves. They are not to advertise themselves as religious over against atheistic enemies

—at least if they cannot show that they are a special, spiritual race.

A look into the past would suggest that America was right "on schedule" as far as worldliness is concerned. By the time it was born people no longer looked at the whole world religiously. Prehistoric man left traces that tell us all of life was magical and religious. Primitive man's relics show that his world was taken up with the life of the gods and spirits. Religious people of the past allowed for no nonsacred laws or ways of life. Both official life and informal manners found them wholly taken up with a divine ordering of their lives. Sometimes Americans try to keep up pretenses, acting as if they were still religious.

Before the nation was born two centuries ago, however, the worlds of primitive and religious humans were shattered. The illusions were passing. The real nature of man as a being at home and still lost in a world was coming to be recognized. More and more people were at war with the gods, determined through science and industry to take control. Some raged against the gods. Others doubted. Still more turned their backs on the heavens and looked to the earth in hope or despair.

Religion was on the defensive when America was established. Few of her people were church members or churchgoers. They had been affected by a trend of centuries. In this trend they separated religious and civil realms, saying in effect that the state could make its way without a formal tie to religion or God. They looked at history less and less as a sphere in which

Providence operated, and more and more as one in which people had mastery. They allowed religion its place, but built a kind of fence around it. In effect, they said, "You may still speak to some things that concern people. We do not care whether or not you talk pie in the sky to them. But leave the world and the running of the world to us."

In such a climate it has always been easy to ignore the stirrings of the spirit. We have had to lay bricks, plow fields, invest capital, speculate with the lives of other peoples. One need only glance at the history to see how consistent this story has been. The Spanish and Portuguese explorers of the Western Hemisphere regularly planted the flags of Catholic majesties and made pious pronouncements about extending God's rule. But they took the gold and the land, raped the women, killed the kings, snatched whatever property interested them, and tried to enslave the people who already lived here. They fought as empires against empires. At best, the name of God was used to justify their imperialism and greed.

When the English-speaking peoples began colonizing, they kept the precedent going. Virginians paid less attention to their Episcopal chaplains and the needs of American Indians than they did to their futile search for gold or northwest passages. They abandoned the mission as soon as it was convenient to do so. Their church was part of a gentleman's way of life, but it did not intrude on business.

Somehow people think of New England settlers as especially pious and spiritual. Their language suggests

that they were. But their behavior shows that they could easily forget or twist the language to make things come out right. They were concerned with status, with economic interests. They came with biblical words that prepared them for failure. When they succeeded they forgot about Providence and talked about progress and practice. The Puritans became Yankees, people of thrift and economic aggressiveness.

In the Middle Colonies, little was different. In New Amsterdam the Calvinists left their ministers behind and arranged life around money, not around divine purpose. The Quakers seemed to be nonworldly, but as they came to earthly success they cheated on themselves; if their wives could not be allowed worldly lace, they came to own the most extravagant linens, which were allowed.

After settlement came a period when new philosophies made their way. People often call this the American Enlightenment; the light of reason and nature was supposed to shape the people. The Enlightenment called people to set their affections on this world, to be at home in it, to have nothing to do with miracles and revelation. Commerce, politics, practical matters took everyone's time. The founding fathers founded a worldly society.

In the nineteenth century there were religious revivals and America surprised the world by building churches along with banks and saloons. But what came forth from the new converts? They used their faith more than ever to amass wealth and justify the na-

tion's policies. They would let God into their private lives, but not into public policies. What did come out of nineteenth-century America? The world would answer: "Yes, you sent missionaries. But you were most concerned with markets. You used the language of religion to have things your own way. Your industrialists were robber barons, using the poor according to their whims and needs." God was pushed to the margins of life.

America produced literary giants, almost none of them Christian or Jewish in any practicing way. They remembered the old faiths, attacked them or transformed them, and then moved beyond them to new myths and stories. By the twentieth century it was difficult to find authors who stood in the nation's religious traditions. But they should not be attacked especially by the pious. Modern American religion has also been very materialistic. Prophets of positive thinking show how Jesus was in the world to help people become rich. Bruce Barton's *The Man Nobody Knows* typified the search in the 1920s: Jesus was a backslapping businessman, a right thinker about the things of this world. Mind-cures, religion used to produce physical health, cults that catered to individual egos, churches devoted to the pursuit of success—all these came to the front.

Some Christians and Jews, of course, tried to counter these trends. But they were a minority, always on the defensive. New religions came to visibility, on the cover of paperback books at airport newsstands. Some of them called for the simple life, for spiritual medita-

tion. More of them offered more things of this world. Even conservative evangelical Christians found it difficult to separate themselves from what Wall Street or the Pentagon wanted for America. The easiest way for any prophet of God to be discredited is to speak out against the worldliness and materialism of the society —and mean it. Anyone can call American preoccupations by bad names; but make any move about changing them and the speaker or actor will be in trouble.

The two-hundred-year-old nation, then, presents the world with a strange mixture. The landscape is still dotted with churches, some of them well-attended and others of them rotting monuments in changing communities. There are still clergy, fund drives, church organizations. In the Congress you can always get votes by saying that you want to put God into the Constitution, since the founding fathers neglected to do so. It is never difficult to get the chaplains (military or civilian) out to bless the cannon. Before the bloody violence of a college or professional football game, someone is usually around to intone a prayer over the proceedings. Beauty contests, dog shows, Little League banquets, service clubs—none of these know how to get their business started without reference to God.

However frequent may be the visible or aural symbols of religious preoccupations, the real business of America remains business. It is taken for granted that prosperity and military success are proper expectations of all truly religious people. The famed nineteenth-century cleric Henry Ward Beecher knew

what he was doing when he attacked the poor for being poor. The people about whom the prophets in the Hebrew Scriptures and Jesus in the Gospels spoke and for whom he said he came are largely overlooked in middle-class American ways. When religion appears, it is usually to justify the status quo. Few ministers would last more than a few weeks if they called into question the terms of American self-seeking.

Rather than make charges about American worldliness, the prophets—all of whom are themselves somehow or other compromised—do well to have people fashion "do it yourself kits" for observation. Anyone can do it. Make a list of the people who are most widely known in society. Are they not sports heroes and entertainment stars who have "made it" and who most represent creeds of success? Name the heroes. How many come from areas of life in which spiritual concerns predominate? For every young person who has focused interest on a spiritual message of a gifted person there will be ten who devote themselves with idolatrous passion to a rock star.

Who interprets American life? Does a lay or clerical leader of a religious group? Or is it the television commentators, the economists, the members of the cabinet, the writers of popular novels—few of whom have any concern for the eternal dimensions of life.

Will there be a slowing down of these trends? Herman Kahn of the Hudson Institute thinks that the future will find the culture more sensate and secular. People in it will ever more turn their backs on divine explanations. They want answers from laboratories

and legislatures, test tubes and defense departments. They will elect people who never challenge them to sacrifice but who minister to their needs for financial and national security. They will be interested in programs, contracts, controls. Such a society allows for people at the margins who remind their contemporaries of the things of the spirit. Each person in such a society may allow for God at the margins of his or her life. But only the foolish would invest in stocks of religion.

These observations, drawn from what foreign visitors see in America, are not intended to be original so much as they are typical. They do not try to go deep to ask about the quality of American worldliness. Some people are discontented after they have piled up status and goods. Others turn selfish and smug. Some are seeking a better way. Why are they so worldly, so materialistic? The answers have to go back to questions about what these citizens share with others: human nature, insecurity, self-centeredness, envy. Americans are not uniquely preoccupied with goods and success. They are fascinating to a larger world because they make a bigger pretense of escaping such selfish interests. They use God's name to obscure the true reality.

The Christian lives his or her life in such a world knowing something about human nature and the causes of its fallen condition and selfishness. The Christian cannot rise wholly above bodily concerns and interests; his faith does not even call him to do this. But anyone in the tradition of biblical faith knows that when

prophets are to be sought, they are not to be found among those who cry "peace, peace" when there is no peace, or among those who permit their brothers and sisters to be at ease in Zion. Americans are to be most faulted when they find religious justifications for their illusions and their worldly ways, when they are content with false prophets who tell them that they are spiritual when they are not.

-2-

Amnesia and Present-Mindedness

RELIGIOUS AMERICA often has historical amnesia. The nation's pious often cannot remember their past, or they show little interest in it. Sometimes they reject the past when it is pointed out to them. What's wrong with that? it may be asked. Some religions of the Eastern world seem to have no sense of the past at all. In them, people seek the timeless, or they follow the rhythms of the year or see meaningless reincarnations in life after life. Some religions of the West have been so weighted down with the past that their practitioners live in the past. They are afraid to make any new moves because they have a burden of tradition. They are contemporary with their ancestors. All the good things happened long ago.

Some Americans have, of course, been influenced by Eastern religions like Buddhism or Hinduism. It is not our business at this point to argue them out of their philosophies, even if we disagree with them. At

this point it is more important to note that America's historic faiths, those derived from the Bible, cannot leave history alone. They are born of a new and different religious sense in which history "moves." God creates a world and will bring it to consummation. In between life has plot and purpose, as God creates and shapes a people and then deals with them in history. For the Christian in particular, in whose vision Jesus Christ is at a center of history, the movement of time has meaning. Not to care about the past, to be a victim of historical amnesia, means that a person will misunderstand biblical faith.

Many Americans go further than mere neglect of the past. Some of them make a point of trying to step outside of history. In the nineteenth century, American literary figures who made up what R. W. B. Lewis in *The American Adam* has called "the party of hope" would say, "forget historical Christianity." They meant: be free for the new. Symbols of the past had had their day and were now exhausted. Those who responded to these were keepers of the dead. In our own time we hear of "now" people, who think that only the present matters, or futurists who act as if we can get a new start—as if we had any images or words that were not colored by past usage. Even some theologians have pretended that they could carry on their work "for the first time" as if the past had not existed.

Aleksandr Solzhenitsyn, the great Russian novelist who was expelled from the Soviet Union, regularly complained that the Soviet government, by not letting him make people aware of the sacrifice of lives in

forced labor camps, was doing violence to history and thus to humanity. The story of suffering must be told, if we are to honor the sufferers. The social psychologist Theodor Adorno speaks in similar terms: tradition represents problems. It is not easily acquired, held to, or understood and can be misused. But to lose tradition is to forget the story and to dishonor past sufferers—and thus to contribute to inhumanity. In the case of Judaism or Christianity, the faith cannot even be held or known unless a story of past events is told, whether or not that story is confined to biblical times.

If history or tradition is lost, people lose their identities. An individual who is afflicted with amnesia does not know who he or she is. In the recent American past there has been much discussion of the effects of mobility and of uprooting from the past. During the days of the Watergate debate many people spoke of the problem of the lack of identity. Harold J. Abramson in an article, "Watergate: Death at the Roots" (*Columbia Forum,* Winter 1974) was typical in his argument that the President and those around him had lost their sense of roots, of ethnicity, and peoplehood, of being responsible to a tradition. Whether or not they were correct in the detailed applications to specific persons (such as former President Richard M. Nixon), these analysts' over-all diagnosis did point to the human problem of identity.

Americans have not found it easy to acquire pasts, traditions, and histories. They were all uprooted from their old homes—whether they were American Indians, Africans, Asians, or Europeans. They came to

a land without monuments or landmarks. They broke the virgin soil and conquered the wilderness. They mingled with people who had somewhat different histories and memories. But through the years many of the religious went out of their way to create identity problems for themselves and to dishonor past sufferers or moral models by trying to forget them.

As a result, much American spirituality has been characterized by a fickle obsession with novelty and fads. If it is new, some say, salute it. The anthropologist Margaret Mead spoke of the psychic damage when she complained that American oldsters were incapable of passing on living histories or traditions. As a consequence their children were forced to have to "make a mish-mash" of all the world's religions and they came up with nothing durable or satisfying.

When a living sense of history is lost, as it often is in American history, people will take a particular moment out of the past and isolate and idolize it. Instead of a moving picture they have a snapshot, which they enshrine. They assume there were once "good old days," from which we have fallen. They oppose all change. But these "good old days" never existed; the historian knows that all days were full of ambiguity and compromise. Or they will be enslaved by a false picture of the past. C. S. Lewis once said that those who do not know history will be victims of recent bad history. Thus many reject religion because they remember bad features of their own childhood faith and never come into contact with remote and other pasts, some of which were livelier and more liberating.

The indictment then runs: Americans are guilty of amnesia, or of rejecting the past, or of idolizing a single moment from a tradition whose flow they do not know, or of suffering under a bad memory because they do not know the larger context. Whoever looks around will find plenty of signs of this strange attitude toward history. While the death of God theologians could be counted on one hand and their followers on another, they represented an intellectual "advance guard's" view that the past did not speak to our believing world. The students who wanted "relevance" in the colleges of the 1960s would not sit still for the telling of the story of faith. Denominations rarely pay much for keeping their story alive; they let universities and historical societies do so but they seem unconcerned with or even afraid of the past.

Some denominations make a snapshot and an idol of the first or the thirteenth centuries, or in some cases the sixteenth. Christians have good reason to be attentive to the century of Jesus Christ and the apostles; but they were emphatic in their argument that they belonged to a long history of God's dealing with his people and that Christians would find their identity only by becoming part of the story of that dealing. For centuries Roman Catholics acted as if God's truth were bound to the way thirteenth-century philosophers thought about him—as if there had been no creative thought before that time or since, or as if those philosophers had a unique and virtually absolute hold on truth.

That perspective on today's religion would also in-

clude a view of people who deal with the past in terms of dogma and not of history. Dogma or doctrine may be a useful human comment on the living acts of God among people. But dogma also chips away the ragged edges of human experience; it plugs all the gaps and holes. It more easily shapes icons and idols. Antihistorical attitudes are also present in the practices of churches, when they show how casually they can reject the pre-American religious pasts, or can bring bulldozer and steel ball to the holy places—rendered holy by the prayerful experience of people—in the American landscape.

All these attitudes that deprive people of identity have a long history, and the problem of anti-past can be understood only by those who will take a moment to look at the past. In colonial America people were often conscious that they were throwing off history. In the wilderness they would have a new start. They no longer felt themselves a part of the struggles of God's people elsewhere. History began anew with them. After they overcame their homesickness they soon lost curiosity about the spiritual record of others. In the case of the slaves, their past was forcibly taken from them by white oppressors who did not allow them their story or their ritual. In New England the repudiation of so much of the past did not mean that people were free for present and future so much as that they took refuge in dogmas or codes. They worshiped what they thought were perfect codes or formulae. The historian Peter Gay tells us that the verb

"to innovate" was the most dirty word one could use in religious circles.

In colonial times, it must be said, there were many who did still keep the historical sense alive. The new problems came with the period shortly after this nation was formed or while it was being formed two centuries ago. Here the political shapers of the nation, the revered founding fathers, can often be faulted. They were naïve about the way in which in the new world they thought they were cutting themselves off from the record of the past and were free to begin afresh. They made their motto *novus ordo seclorum,* the idea that they were bringing in a "new order of ages." They had a passion for novelty, and wanted to live off only the philosophy and science of their own day or off ideas about government and about the universe that they themselves would dream up.

In the first half of the nineteenth century Americans of this "enlightened" tradition began to reacquire a sense of history; "romantic nationalists," as they were called, began to tell the American story. But they did this by repudiating the Christian and Western past. They might pay lip service to the contributions of an isolated European hero, but after passing mention they turned to American forests and waterfalls for drama and wisdom. Historian David Noble has even argued that Americans who write about the past are *Historians against History.* They were so sure of themselves and what their times could offer that they turned their backs on the longer human record. When

they preached their "jeremiads"—and he thinks they did preach as America's semi-secular theologians—they attacked Americans for failing to listen to the lessons of nature and for wanting to acquire a past, a tradition.

The transcendentalist poets and essayists, the Emersons and Thoreaus and Parkers and many of the articulators of the romantic vision of America like Walt Whitman were—to use the not always fortunate slang of a later age—"now" people. They celebrated the present moment and scourged all who lived in or with the past. Few would deny the liberating side of some of their proclamations. They knew that tradition misused could kill. But they in effect were also helping amputate their contemporaries, cutting off something vital to humanity.

Can America's Christians look at these enlightened and romantic forefathers and say that they themselves have always understood the importance of looking at the human, the Christian, the American pasts as milieux or landscapes in which God's saving activity is unfolding? It is hard to generalize because there have been so many varieties of religious experience in America. But two examples of religious emphases that deprived people of a lively sense of the past can be accented. Both of them, let it be said, often exemplified virtues that some other Christians lacked; but they also created fresh problems for understanding faith and identity.

The first of these two are often called the advocates of "the primitive Gospel." These frontier people were

rightfully disgusted about debates over traditions and handed-down practices. They were exhausted by the debates between competing denominations and felt that these debates were caused by misreadings of histories. They would start from scratch and, out of all the aeons of history, would take one generation as their source and model. This generation was—who would deny it? —a valuable one for Christians, for in it Jesus lived and in it he called his disciples. But the primitivists or restorationists often acted as if God's dealing with his people had been obscured again until the time of the American frontier nineteen centuries later. All that mattered was an individual's immediate experience of conversion and revival; the only past that would reach him was a codified version of the first Christian century. As refreshing as some of this emphasis was on the religious scene, it helped create problems for people who had to wrestle with questions of how God acts in history, and who his people are.

On the other hand, many continental immigrants, whether Roman Catholic, Lutheran, or Reformed, looked as if they brought pasts and living traditions with them. But as they embraced American life many of them also forgot that they belonged to history and rigidified their thought in doctrine and liturgy, both of which were used to help people try to escape history. When anything happened that looked like a challenge to these out-of-context dogmas, faith itself seemed to be compromised or threatened.

The natural forces of American life took their toll of the "primitives" and the "dogmatists" as well as of

those who somewhere between them tried to be responsive to the meaning of the past as a springboard to true innovation and meaningful change. The Industrial Revolution swept people up from the valleys and countrysides where they could preserve social and religious memories and jammed them into cities. They were moved whenever their services were needed elsewhere. Their children had no reference points of the kind people in traditional societies had. In the twentieth century the great suburban move in the midst of an affluent society served further to dislocate people. Pluralism, the reality of many religions of many peoples in close contact with each other, made it a problem for people to gain identities and to pass on values.

Many of these are inevitable problems; the tragedy in a spiritual sense occurs when religious people do not creatively face the issue, when they add to it by forgetting or repudiating the history of which they are a part and from which they are to draw hopes for the future.

-3-

The Lonely
Individualist

MODERN LIFE is full of forces that make people lonely.
These forces are intensified in the United States. In
nations where people spend their lives in one village or
country valley, it is easy for them to build community.
They all know their place. The people around them
serve as reference points. Attend a wedding in the
countryside of any traditional society—or a leftover
quiet community in America—and you will see a much
different ritual than the one that goes on at most urban
American marriages. In the old village wedding, everyone present would know all the members of both
families. Their parents have known each other. The
bridal pair will spend their lives in the same place.
The important happenings in their life will be recognized by everyone around them.

In America, the people who marry probably have
met at a college in a different state. They have come
home for the weekend; after the honeymoon they will

move where the two can find employment. From then on, they will at best make a two-day or two-week stop at the home of the bride's or groom's parents—and these stops may neither give them roots nor company, since these parents like one out of five other Americans last year may have moved. At the wedding, then, the people on the two sides of the aisle have never seen each other before and will not come into contact again. Many who are there are invited for business reasons or out of a sense of social obligation. Faces come and go; the champagne flows; empty chatter follows; people pass each other in the aisles or on the ballroom floor. Then they make their way out into the night, to their automobiles, airports, and lonelinesses.

Fifty years later the couple will be found living in a retirement city, cut off from whatever roots they developed through the years. Or one will have died, leaving the other away from family in a nursing home. No one calls and no one cares. Tenements and apartments are full of the lonely. One student of the city has said that you can kill a person as well with an apartment as with an axe or a gun; it only takes a little longer.

Loneliness and isolation are simply part of the modern condition, a condition intensified in America. Religious America can hardly be faulted for sharing with the rest of the world a natural and inevitable problem. The question of fault and blame comes in at two points. One does not concern us here; this has to do with whether religionists are doing all they can to minimize individual separation and minister to those alone. The matter that is our subject here is more

critical: Does religious America build into its way of life and then sanction with piety a pattern that pits lonely people against each other? Has American individualism proven to be destructive of human community and spiritual values?

Even the hint or the smell of an attack on individualism has an overtly anti-American sound to it. The idea that the individual matters most is a cherished idea in our society. Certainly there are biblical bases for such thinking. The Scriptures talk frequently about the merit and worth of each person. God creates each, cares for them, rescues them, and makes them responsible again. The Hebrew Scriptures expect a response to God from each individual. In the New Testament Jesus Christ dies for the sinner, for each one. Personal decision about his claim is expected.

But, all this occurs as part of the community. Little religious value is associated in historic Christianity with the idea of the individual off by himself or herself, competing against all others, often in the name of God. This competition can occur in both the material and the spiritual realms. The Dean of Harvard Divinity School, Krister Stendahl, has effectively argued that American Christians have often twisted biblical concerns. Their kind of salvation-talk is egocentric: "What are you doing for *me,* God; who cares what happens to the larger community?" It focuses entirely on the doctrine of salvation; being rescued is more important than building the created world or serving others. "Are you saved?" "Did you accept Jesus

Christ as your personal Savior?" These questions are not entirely inappropriate. But they are made into an American creed, one which forgets that in biblical faith people are saved *with* people and with *a* people; God creates and shapes, guides and redeems Israel.

From the biblical points of view, then, American isolation or individualism with their accompanying competition serves to complicate problems of loneliness and selfishness. A canvass of the surrounding world shows how much this ideology separates Americans from the rest of the human race.

Most world religions do not even have the choice of separating persons from the larger community in order to save them. They exist in failure-cultures, not success-cultures. They have to be designed to show people how to cope with misery and not to justify achievement and comfort. This is not to say that other religions do not have sects and parties or separate traditions. But it is rare for them to make their claims on the basis of what they can do for the individual in isolation.

When Christians moved out into the larger world their isolation and individualism marked their mission, too. Missions became a competitive game. While virtually all Christians believe that the reconciling circle in Jesus Christ should grow, few of them have counted what destruction occurs for persons who are brought to faith through biblical slogans apart from the memories of nations, tribes, and families. Many stories of Christian missions, especially to Jews, are set in individual competitive terms. A Jew is an especially good

catch. I must snatch him from everything that makes him a person and give him a slogan or formula that will save him. Then I pay no more attention to him. I send missionaries who infiltrate the worshiping centers of other faiths and spiritually kidnap individuals from them. "My God is better than your gods," becomes the implied slogan. Yet how resentful we are when we are treated in kind and an occasional Buddhist or Hindu makes a pitch for individual converts on our soil. We play by two sets of rules.

A third illustration of how American religion works for loneliness and individualism has to do with how it is projected over mass media of communication. Radio or television shows beamed into small apartments of shut-ins no doubt have creative purposes. But they also create the impression to the non-shut-in that here is a substitute for the life of a gathered community. Why bother to share each other's burdens when one can listen to the guru of his choice while nibbling a TV dinner and staring out the window? Why bother as long as I am receiving Jesus as my "personal" Savior?

Finally, catholicity is obscured in all this. By catholicity we mean the sense that our faith has to do with the whole past and points to the whole community. Our individualism makes personal decision the whole issue, without reference to the witness of faithful sufferers through the ages who in community passed on the tradition, the Scripture, the faith. People are saved by dogmas that suit each of them. They repudiate Europe, Africa, Asia, or wherever the believing community

had lived. We despair of true community and live unto ourselves.

For all the benefits that go with the voluntary system in church life ("go to the church of your choice"), there is also a toll in the loss of religious symbols to support larger community. We do not know how to discuss morals or values in the midst of political scandal, educational traumas, or national upheaval, since there are no agreed-upon terms or boundaries for the discussion. Professors Sidney E. Mead and Robert N. Bellah have often spoken of the need for a "religion of the republic." This need not imply worship of the nation. Instead it would represent a place where all the people could face each other in the spirit of at least some consensus, as they determined the truth for them, and the questions of national destiny.

Even where a kind of self-critical and transcendent religion that has to do with national community emerges, it is immediately broken down by the competitive ways in which people grasp it: as Jews, Catholics, or black or white Protestants of 250 different greedy breeds or brands—each of them standing by with a private interpretation for each individual.

If religious ideas compromise national community, so religious denominations are destructive of national community. The denomination is jerry-built to cater to the individual more than to be expressive of the church. It allows for the holding of private truth by "the right of private judgment" without reference to others. "You do things your way, and I'll do things God's way," is the way this is usually put. Individual-

ism and competition are at the heart of denomination-alism. People pick and choose truths as if on a cafe-teria line, until they get the right diet or mixture.

As with denominations, so with parishes, congrega-tions, synagogues, or other local worship centers. In many cases these are the result of competition. You "drop in" casually at the church of your choice. It is not a natural community of believers so much as an ex-pression of the individual self according to the acci-dents of locale or economic position. The supportive faith of a community beyond the local congregation is forgotten.

The pursuit of loneliness and the support of com-petitive isolated individualism, also in religion, has a long history in America. Long before the founding of the nation two centuries ago the fathers disposed their heirs to have the problem of disrupted community. Some of the colonists called themselves "separatists." Admirably courageous and consistent though they may have been—and no one wants to take away from them the clarity of their vision or the sacrifices they under-went to live it out—they created problems for descend-ants. The separatist spirit counters the claims of Christ's community-building spirit for all Christians. What is more, even in the nonseparatist colonies, those who participated soon found that the message bred individualism. The Puritan preacher concen-trated more and more on the personal "heart pre-pared." The preaching of revival was designed to ac-cent what a person had to achieve all alone, almost by an act of will.

The nineteenth century saw an accentuation of all these problems. The revivalist more and more pitched himself at the rescue of the individual apart from the community. In colonial times the call was still for the "owning of the covenant" for the good of the larger community. But that bred a sense of spiritual pride. If I accept the pitch, then I am superior to all the mortals who have not made the same act of private judgment. When I interpret the Scriptures "my way," I am no longer bound to be responsible to others. When I support my denomination in its outreach, I can take my models from the business community. Most justifications of sectarianism draw not at all on biblical support. Almost all of them point to the advantages—some of them apparent—of having competitive preachers and tract-handlers competing so that every kind of option might be offered and more individuals will find something to their liking.

At bicentennial time it is proper to ask about the legacy of such an ideology and approach. Here revivalism has reached into almost any kind of faith, including those that never were shaped by evangelism. Mass evangelism or life in larger parishes does provide people with a sense of being part of a movement. But they find themselves needed chiefly as statistics and to provide support. The message has to do with what God can do for them if they play along with each of them. A curious contradiction or paradox results. We are a nation of joiners, yet seem pathetically lonely. We have ideologies of sharing, yet go our own ways. The political scientist Sebastian de Grazia asks what hap-

pens to young persons who find themselves in the face of competing claims. Our national life and our religious life tell us two opposite things. We must cooperate completely. And we must compete completely. The adolescent becomes confused and weary and drops out of the struggle.

The cities do much to accent the religiously justified individualism. While some historians call aspects of the thesis into question, most agree with people like Richard Sennett that the family has had to bear too much of the weight of community and has therefore broken apart and produced more alienation. In the past people lived in tribes, in extended families that brought together grandmother or grandfather with cousins and kin. When they moved to the city they settled by pushing a couple of parents and several children under one roof. They had no intimate reference points. They might go to a church, but they passed eight other churches on the way to it. They had to make things work in too small a cell; families clawed and scratched at each other, until only the psychiatrists prospered.

If there is any place that has been romanticized by the defenders of American rugged individualism, also in religion, it is the frontier. In the nineteenth-century West, we are told, enterprising John Wayne types left behind the false securities of groups. They struck out on their own. They learned mastery of the soil and lived with the sky and the seasons. They gouged deeper and deeper into hills for gold and silver. Because they were ahead of or beyond the law, they became vigi-

lantes and took the law into their own hands. They enjoyed being beyond the range of others and welcomed isolation. That picture is placed before schoolchildren as something they should aspire to copy.

Never. For one thing, they live in a world of crowds and computers, time clocks and assembly lines. They have no place to hide. For another, the frontiersmen did not themselves live such splendidly chosen lives of isolation, nor did they cherish their loneliness. The diaries of pioneer women find most of them desperately left to themselves, in dreary and meaningless lives. They should not all be faulted; the economic situation and the state of invention at the time left them no choice. But they and their improvised religious responses hardly serve as models for people who have to overcome loneliness, competition, isolation, and rugged individualism.

The suburbs are the new frontiers for the new lonely people. The crack in the picture window, the ticky-tacky housing, the ever-present moving van, the frantic cocktail party have all come to symbolize what one scholar has called "the eclipse of community." It does not pay to complain about what is inevitable in a way of life, insofar as that way of life is necessary for survival. But it is valid for the self-consciously religious to ask whether they have done little more than to make matters worse by writing creeds and myths that defend rugged individualism and play down the community of the whole "people of God." The philosopher Alfred North Whitehead said (though in a context that is quite often forgotten) that religion is what a

person does with his solitariness. In biblical religion it has to do with what he does with community. American religion made Whitehead's definition understandable and placed biblical definition almost beyond reach.

-4-

Provincialism and Nationalism

THE LOVE of country that can produce much good by developing identity and giving people a place in the world can also be perverted when too much religious justification is applied. If anyone needs proof that the mixture between religion and nationalism or peoplehood can be dangerous, he or she need only look around at a world of late twentieth-century tensions. Almost all the wars of our time are holy wars. In the Asian subcontinent Hindus in India constantly fight border warfare with Muslims in Pakistan—when they are not in rioting situations with Muslims within India. In Southeast Asia different kinds of Buddhists and Roman Catholics warred with other kinds of Buddhists and non-Catholics. The Vietnamese War cannot be described simply on religious lines, but religion played its part.

Religious nationalism is even more visible and acute in the world's most dangerous trouble spot. In the Mid-

dle East Jews have religious ideas about the tie between their faith and the land of Israel. Meanwhile Arabs, united by little except a common love of Allah and hatred of Israel, are always in hot or cold war situations with that smaller land—inspired by a sense, at times, of *jihad* or holy war that permits people to die for sacred causes—and to kill for the same. Lest American Christians point fingers, they have to be reminded that the economic and social tensions in Northern Ireland are heightened by Protestant and Catholic religious identifications of the sniping and warring parties. In African tribal warfare religious symbols and claims accompany the efforts of both contenders.

Not all problems of this type result in open warfare. It is possible that far short of shooting, religious provincialism can build mistrusts, suspicions, and hatreds that distort people's views of themselves and of others. At the very least they will think of themselves as being the special darlings of destiny. They will lose regard for people in other circumstances. At worst they may come to believe that they have a special arrangement with God and are free to carry on a mission, perhaps even one that leads to domination, anywhere in the world. The kind of temptation associated with this missionary sense comes especially to powerful and pretentious nations.

Such provincialism distorts a motif that most religions regard as being legitimate. That is, most of them want to take care lest their people consider the drama of faith to be enacted only in a distant cloudland. These faiths indicate reasons for caring about

one's own people and place. But almost all of them—
and Christianity is particularly emphatic on this point
—move beyond such localism and suggest that the God
of nations cannot be tied down to the fate and pride of
a single nation or people or valley. Not only is this a
theological matter about doctrines and Scriptures, it
has immediate and direct human and humane consequences. People who are too cozy and intimate about
their relations to God can assert dominance over others
or can neglect them. They will fail to share benefits
with others, and will have little sense of sympathy
with the less fortunate. Others will be judged by the
standards of the folks who are sure that God is on
their side.

With that background, the person who turns his eye
on the American present and past can see a record of
countless failings. These failings would be harmless
in remote little nations in the eddies and bypaths of
history. But when one of the two or three most powerful nations in the world—as the United States has
been for many decades—links up with divine purpose
to charter its ways among the nations, the potential
for trouble is truly great. It is possible to tell the story
of American religious provincialism in two ways: one
can begin with a jeremiad, a scolding of the nation as
a whole for its military and imperial manners. Or it
can begin on a more intimate scale; sometimes that can
be more revelatory.

Provincialism shows up in American religionists'
passion for their own front yards, their own neigh-
borhoods or precincts—no matter what the shape of

the larger world may be. Writers often like to reduce world statistics to comprehensible numbers. For example, they will divide the population and resources of the world by some figure or other to be able to picture America as a village in a state called the world. Then they show what percentage of the products of technology—telephones and automobiles and the like—are used by Americans. They come up with dramatic figures about the way people in the United States consume huge proportions of the world's energy and disproportionate amounts of its food. The telling effect of all this is to show that Americans often forget their good fortune and have little sense of what being homeless and hungry, poor and revolutionary is.

The problem is often intensified in religion, where the local church has such dominance in people's minds. While they may profess a Christian style of faith, which makes so much of the love of all and of Christ's work for people throughout history and in all parts of the world, they rarely look beyond their pocketbooks, their noses, their sanctuaries. The part of the charitable dollar that goes beyond expenses for local religious institutions is very small. Concern is low. While a returning missionary may be exotic enough to attract some attention, ordinarily if a congregation programs something about human need at any distance, it is not likely to draw a crowd.

Prejudicial attitudes parallel these practices. American Christians have great difficulty listening to those who have different circumstances. Thus when representatives of younger churches in developing nations

engage in any kind of critique of capitalism or free enterprise or of the way of life that has made America
prosperous—even if sometimes these criticisms are
misguided or ill-founded in part—they are not heard.
Or they are militantly rejected. When the World Council of Churches or the Vatican Council of the Roman
Catholic Church or any other truly ecumenical (universal, world-wide) forum makes room for representatives of the Third World, American Christians
of many political stripes resist by saying these speakers are all "a bunch of communists." No one takes
time to hear whether or not they might also be fellow-
Christians, people who are far from accepting all the
antireligious corollaries of communism and Marxism,
but who also cannot build their societies on the principles and practices Americans have enjoyed.

While the reference to local self-interest may strike
home and may be something about which believing citizens can do something, it is not possible to postpone
very long the larger-scale and more potent kind of
provincialism in its bond with religion. Modern nationalism almost always comes with religious trappings The late historian Carlton J. H. Hayes once
wrote a book called *Nationalism: A Religion*. In it he
traced the ways in which in the modern world there
are special temptations to connect God and nation or
even to make the nation into a kind of God. This tie is
somewhat different from historic views of promised
lands or holy cities. In the modern world nationalism
is often based on very artificial concepts. Somehow,
usually as the result of a war, people of a certain clus-

ter of racial and ethnic groups find themselves in a new set of boundaries. They have some languages, some shared history; but most of all they are a political and military fabrication.

Immediately they have to find an ideology to justify their life together and to give them a sense of identity. In no time at all a kind of religion develops. They make an icon or an idol out of a flag—as Americans often are capable of doing. They have sacred scenes and shrines; tombs of unknown soldiers are inspirers of a religious vision of nationhood. Elaborate ceremonies are taught in the schools, which become the established churches of the national religion. God is the God of battles, who sides with our side and blesses our cannon against any enemy—even if that enemy may have been minding its own business or even if it was and will be our friend. During the time of enmity, it is seen as living under a "foreign devil."

Further proof that modern nationalism has a religious character can be seen from the way people use it to determine orthodoxy and heresy, loyalty and treason. Once upon a time churches could excommunicate and actually rule someone out of society. Today it is difficult for religious groups to rule anyone out or to limit their freedom. But even a slight deviation from a nation's orthodoxy can lead to exile or punishment. If a Methodist violates church law and crosses a boundary to join Roman Catholicism, he will be warmly received a year later if he comes back home. If the same young person crosses a boundary against civil law and goes to Canada to protest a war he con-

siders immoral, he cannot come home. Something holy has been transgressed. A "man without a church" suffers nothing socially. A "man without a country" has no identity, no basis for faith.

America is not by any means unique in its tendencies to turn the nation into the bearer or the object of religion. But it has special temptations based on its power and the plausibility that goes with its many historic successes. Sociologist Will Herberg argued that Americans were especially provincial in the way that they idolized and lived or died for "the American way of life." Religious conservatives are not the only ones guilty of this. Liberal thinkers have often tried to make up what theologian J. Paul Williams called and advocated as "the religion of democracy," in which the social process itself was a kind of church and its achievements made up a religion.

That America should fall into these temptations is doubly tragic because it is a nation that for two centuries has had special reasons for seeing itself as a part of the family of man. The nation that receives people from Africa, Asia, and especially Europe in wave after wave of forced or chosen immigration; one that has had the affluence to send its students and travelers abroad; the country that most develops means of transportation and communication—such a place ought to be especially empathic. But the "ugly American" came to be seen as the tourist who is impatient about the ways of others and intolerant about what he sees. Seldom are American approaches to the world changed positively as a result of the interactions.

The long history behind American provincialism shows that as people entered the new world they were so taken up with its promise that they often forgot the situation from which they came. Historian David Noble has shown how in the nineteenth century the historians became the Jeremiahs. They developed extremely negative views of Europe. Europe was the place where there were long and confining traditions; there was complexity. America was full of riches and promise in an abundant nature. Behind them, as one poet put it, were "dead kings and remembered sepulchres." Spiritually they often largely cut themselves off from the rest of the world, including even their fellow believers elsewhere.

Traces of the old Spanish cultures of California or Florida were covered up by the founding people of the new "Protestant" nation, for these were too Catholic. At first these Protestants were isolated from each other in their separate colonies. But when they were combined in a nation they took to nationalism with a vengeance. While the War between the States tested this nationalism, it only served more than before to tie God down to regions and parties. President Abraham Lincoln had to try to rise above all of this as "the theologian of the American experience" when he reminded North and South that both sides prayed to the same God and read from the same Bible and expected to win and claimed God for their causes. They should instead have tried to see how they might conform to God's own mysterious purposes, not to claim him for their own.

The Civil War divisions aside, the nineteenth century found the churches devoting themselves ever more to the "manifest destiny" and mission of America in the world. If they sent out missionaries for the churches, these were usually expected to spread along with the Gospel the virtues of American civilization and the manners of the super race of Anglo-Saxons who had created it. But it was not the missionary impulse—however condescending and disruptive it could be at its worst—that was most dangerous in the field of manifest destiny.

More harmful was a kind of imperialism that developed out of the American sense that God had endowed this place with special meaning and mission. America became a "Redeemer Nation." Its aggressions in the Mexican War and the Spanish-American War are well-documented misapplications of the redeemer motif and misuses of other nations.

In the twentieth century imperialism has been more economic than political. Despite the criticisms of communist nations, America has taken over little new land in the globe. But given its economic motivations and momentum its representatives were often capable of trying to serve as policemen to the world, and would interfere with the internal affairs of other nations in order to protect American investments and interests. While it is true that such expansionism is the result of economic concerns, it has largely been endorsed and supported by the religious people who justify any sort of policy because of America's special arrangement with deity.

American nationalism may be entering a new stage, and religious people are less sure than they were before the Vietnamese War just how to tie together the God of battles and American purpose. But their inner uncertainty has not led to visible repentance or a clear expression of desire to be more understanding of other nations. There has been significant retreat from missions and from ecumenism, from anything that would promote closer contact across oceans. A new religious isolationism has tended to make Americans less curious about what goes on elsewhere and less mindful of the reasons why so many take the courses they do. America is not alone in binding God to place and people, but it is a nation of people who profess that God is lord of nations and that no tribe can claim him uniquely as their own.

Part II
The American People

~ 5 ~

The Religiously Prejudiced People

NOWHERE in the world is there a greater variety of religions and opinions living side by side as in America —often with the potential for erupting into ugliness. Drive into any town and you will be confronted by a series of signs competing for attention. Come to the Baptist, Methodist, Catholic, Lutheran, or Christian Science churches. In some smaller communities the spirit of good will has reached far enough that the churches at least chip in financially and buy a common sign. "The churches of Smithville welcome you." But they list themselves separately. Each sends an agent in the path of the Welcome Wagon to see whether a new family can be signed up before it falls into the clutches of a less-than-true religious organization.

The offense can run deeper. Often three or four styles of Baptist churches or Lutheran organizations compete for attention. The tensions between these may often be most intense of all; no one fights like brothers

and cousins. However casual many members of these groups may be, their very existence recalls battles born of intolerance. They continue to lead separate lives not only out of habit and custom but because they at least quietly look down on or are intolerant of their competitors in spiritual matters.

The yellow pages of a phone book or *The Yearbook of the Churches of the United States and Canada* only underscore the alternatives. From one point of view these varieties are attractive; they show that people have cared enough about religion to celebrate its differences. From still another aspect, they represent a problem only for Christian ecumenism: How can people profess one Lord and still go so many separate ways? Neither of these is the concern of this chapter. Instead, we shall concentrate on the ways in which these different embodiments tear at the fabric of neighborly life, produce inconvenience and intolerance, and are counterproductive of religious values.

On two fronts in particular the intolerance erupts. When one group has a different concept of its relation to the whole civil society than does another, ugliness comes forth. The most common illustration is the history of battles between Roman Catholics and other Americans over "the separation of church and state." On this scene great prejudices have served to produce falsehood and bad relations. Many Protestants keep a watchful eye lest any public funds somehow find their way to Roman Catholic elementary or secondary schools—schools often founded because in the nineteenth century, public schools were kind of a junior

Protestant "established church" that taught creeds contrary to Catholic taste. Let a Catholic child get on a public school bus or accept a tax-supported lunch or use a textbook on secular subjects not paid for by Catholic funds, and there is outcry and hue.

Meanwhile, with rare exceptions, the Protestants do not have the courage to examine their own convictions. The complaining groups often accept public funds for dormitories or science buildings on their campuses of higher education. Is there a magical mysterious age-level beyond which the line of separation can be crossed? Or—since we are aware of cases where church groups do not accept such public funds—they do welcome tax exemption. Tax exemption probably pays off more positively for American churches, with their $80 billion worth of property, than does open subsidy where established churches survive, as in Europe. Or they work to establish prayer in public schools, even though formulas cannot be found that will be welcomed by all groups.

If that is one area of intolerance, another has to do with the attitudes toward groups that do not accept the terms of national consensus. Because Americans have grown casual about creed and have found ways to use denominations to neutralize many kinds of conflict, they create the impression that their tolerance of diversity has become nearly boundless. Yet the tolerance exists within a rather carefully defined and corralled context. Most of the tolerant people are intolerant of Jehovah's Witnesses, whose creed tells them that a flag is an idol of a false god who should not be wor-

shiped. They are prejudiced against Witnesses, Hutterites, or others who refuse military service. They try to send governmental agents into cornfields to round up black-hatted suspendered little Amish children whose parents provide separate and "substandard" schools. They resent Quakers and others who provide values for conscientious objection to military service. They are intolerant of dissenting ministers, nuns, priests, rabbis, when these call into question the regular patterns of national life. They are prejudiced against Black Muslim attempts to develop a para-discipline, as in many penitentiaries.

Some of these prejudices are even subtler, and follow class lines. People in main line churches find that their middle-class values are supported by religious groupings, and they are snobbish toward "hillbilly" religion or the spiritual life of ethnic Catholics, Appalachian Protestants, or black ghetto dwellers. Conversely, many of the evangelistic people who have experienced fervent conversions are intolerant of people who have come to God in other ways. Sometimes these intolerances are destructive of personal relationships; at other times they are reflected in public policies that hurt someone. These show up in tax laws, codes having to do with military service, or voting by religious blocs that reflect prejudice.

In the light of the past, it might be said that America has done much to reduce the ugliness of religious opposition. It is true that the history of holy wars shows uglier pasts. Reports of the way in which "the people of God" in Israel were allowed to take their at-

titudes onto the battlefield have been used to justify latter-day persecution. In Christian-Muslim conflicts, the *jihad* and the crusade both served to bring out the ugliest in humans. Crusaders gloried in their accounts of how they waded in pools of enemy blood in order to secure the holy places of the Holy Land for the faithful, out of range of the infidel. In the Christian West the stories have not been pleasant, either. Right up to the time of the settlement of America, in the Thirty Years War or the Puritan Revolution, people regularly used the sword to try to settle matters of creed or to give expression to the narrowness of their own vision. Over against that past, America has come some measure.

Today's situation leaves people with less to brag about than they may think they have; one must look under the surface to see how power is truly lined up on the front of religious prejudice. First, it must be said, Americans have a gift for hiding the dead bodies that grew out of religious conflict. Whoever spoke a good word for the beliefs and values of the native Americans, the Indians, who were killed "in the name of God"? It is possible to segregate spatially the people whose values we least enjoy, or to force self-segregation on them. The Hutterites are in colonies in South Dakota; the Amish are off to themselves in Pennsylvania; the black storefront churches are confined to ghetto streets. We remove from vision those who are not close to the American consensus wherein tolerance is to lie.

It must also be said that much intolerance is covered

up by superficial practices. Because Religion in American Life, an independent agency supported by advertising councils, makes going to "the church of your choice" a plausible slogan, it is implied that America does truly endorse all religious expressions. It is questionable whether R.I.A.L. or military people or others who adopt that slogan really do not care what religious opinions others hold. They assume that chosen churches will be part of the agreed upon favored groups.

Another evidence that all is not well is seen in the need Americans have to use bad humor as escape valves for tense situations. The wearisome minister-priest-rabbi jokes are a good instance. A jokester sidles up to someone, "Have you heard the latest one about . . . ?" The listener has heard it, of course, but allows the speaker to go ahead knowing that it is important to show that tolerance between religious groups exists, as the humor gives evidence. The priests joked about are always harmless duffers. No gentle humor exists about the Berrigan brothers, or the Vietnam War-dissenting rabbis and ministers.

Any study of American religious intolerance also has to face the issue of attitudes toward the nonreligious. Formal atheism is relatively rare in America; it is easier to ignore than to defy the gods. But whenever someone sticks up his or her head in defiance of approved religious canons, the religious righteous become enraged. President Theodore Roosevelt called Thomas Paine a "filthy little atheist," even though the Revolutionary pamphleteer was not filthy nor little nor

atheistic. He simply stood outside the approved boundaries. Where the antagonism most shows up is in the field of politics. In the 1960 campaign, candidate Richard M. Nixon, legitimately trying to remove pressure from the anti-Catholic issue, said that religion would be a point of controversy only should one candidate be an atheist. Should it be? The American charters of political life, from the Constitution to oaths for immigrants, make no such claims. They have to lie in the field of practice, behavior, tolerances, and prejudices.

In practice, the rules of the game are changed constantly for various groups. We have already mentioned inhibitions against many sects freely living out their creeds. The intolerances are apparent on other levels. Those who are for a Prayer Amendment are insensitive to the interests of minorities. If prayers are to be established in public schools can they be truly nonsectarian in outlook? Even postures (folding hands and bowing heads) are associated with separate and competing traditions. On the other hand, have those who have been against prayer in schools been mindful of the religious sympathies of majorities?

The fact that brotherhood organizations have been necessary illustrates the presence of American intolerance. These are supported half-heartedly. One gets the impression that religious leaders are taking part much the way football or hockey club owners share edgy conviviality during the week of their league meetings. After the niceties have been expressed, they go outside and beat each other's brains out again as

before. Countless gestures underscore the tenuous ties of brotherhood. In the right club the right dig at the right time conveys prejudice. At such moments the philosophies of tolerance and the brotherhood organizations all fade.

The customs and practices described here have long histories in America. Commonly held beliefs suggest that our forefathers came to these shores to give expression to religious toleration. With few exceptions that myth has no basis in fact. They came for religious freedom to go their own way. Others had perfect freedom not to come to their colonies, or to stay away, or to leave the moment their minds changed. Banishment from a colony was one form of expressing intolerance. In New England seacoast towns sailors were carefully kept from contact beyond the harbor. They were strangers, with threatening outsiders' religious values. Merchants could not always be trusted, because their commerce brought them into contact with value systems that the rulers of colonies did not want to have represented even temporarily.

The colonists were generally quite prejudiced against religions other than their own; where they could, as in nine of thirteen colonies, they established and required support of a particular church. Dissenters were unwelcome. As years passed it was necessary for compromises to be made. The change toward toleration came more from practical necessity than from religious bases. And those who expressed regard for others still had limited vision. Most colonies insisted on Protestant or Trinitarian creedal confession on the part of their

public officials. They saw nothing wrong with total denial of the values and rights of their American Indian contemporaries, and systematically deprived black slaves of their "inferior" inherited and imported African beliefs.

While some colonists used religion to bring about change in attitudes, the limits were often very narrow. Even the "enlightened" statesmen like Thomas Jefferson could be very intolerant. What he said about the beliefs of Calvinists is hardly expressive of a truly open mind. He was, of course, a man of his time. And he had good reason to criticize the sectarians for their bickering and the established churches for suppressing the freedom of others. But his faith in the new philosophies led him to dismiss too readily and too vehemently the claims of Christian faith, and he resolved to do what he could to put the churches in their place. He was not alone. Whatever results came from the new legal way in America, in practice majorities only have extended as much sense of tolerance as they found necessary.

The nineteenth century offers many ugly tales. On the southwest frontier Protestants tried to do each other in, and tried to ward off developments of new groups. In Boston and Philadelphia Protestants burned Catholic convents. Riots in the streets pitted Protestants against Catholics. The religion of the Eastern Orthodox or the Jews was despised, and that of blacks was ruled out or redefined by white masters.

Twentieth-century "pluralism" suggests improvements. But Protestant reaction to the idea of a Roman

Catholic ambassador or some of the Catholic rhetoric against birth control or abortion has often served to inflame more than to inform. Jewish-Christian relations remain tense, particularly when matters affecting differing policies on Israel come up. Studies of religious textbooks have shown much covert anti-Semitism in Christian books.

So far as the future is concerned, we may expect continued tensions to exist between majorities and minorities, between those who express the consensus faiths versus those who dissent. America has going for it the mere fact that its founders were weary of actual holy war. They had seen too much bloodshed. The fact that religious groups give at least half their hearts to the world and simply do not care all that much has been another factor in their favor. The presence in the 1970s of so many exotic and extravagant-appearing new maverick groups in religion has made it possible for many once-outrageous appearing minority groups to look more conventional and acceptable.

When other interests are tested American intolerance comes into play. Denominations seem to be inventions that exist to drain off bloody conflict into harmless channels. Who cares whether someone baptizes at one age through one means or another? People no longer fight in the political realm over definitions of the Trinity. But let religion be even vaguely related to other points of controversy, especially those that touch on the pocketbook or the military policies, and all the latent old uglinesses reappear. Ask any dissenter or member of a minority.

-6-

A Racist Nation

AMERICA is a racist nation. No charge against it carries more weight or passion from the nations of the world than that one. Whoever thought that American religious intolerance was an embarrassment or inconvenience has to know that racial hatred has cost thousands of lives and ruined millions more. Neither the hated nor the hater is a truly free person, and the nation built upon such hatred is constantly threatened.

The American majority is white and gentile. This, however, represents a tiny minority in a world of many different races. Most of these people are poor, living in underdeveloped nations; they are resentful of American wealth and pride, reactive against the United States' expansionist spirit, observant of its inner life. Nothing is more offensive than the way the nation builds so much of its life, beginning with its housing policies and practices and carrying over into almost every other realm, on lines of race.

Agreed, one can picture the reader saying. But why should this topic show up in a book on bicentennial assessments of American religiosity? Let religion take

care of itself and let racial concerns find their own areas for experts. The problem is that they overlap. Much religion and, notably, much American religion is very closely related to racial ways of looking at the world. And racial hatred or concord are both usually supported by religious claims.

No one knows quite why. People have been studying race relations for centuries and they have been giving special attention to it in a time when racial wars threaten the whole human family. The more scientists, sociologists, anthropologists, or psychologists study the issue the more mysterious it seems to be. Somehow, somewhere deep in the practices if not the nature of humans there seems to be a need to identify one's self through some sort of "natural" skein. The nation helps many grasp a universe. But the nation is partly artificial. Religion helps, but does not serve for everything. One's race seems so integral to one's personality and place in the world that it has a mysterious hold that few transcend. And when a hold is mysterious, it is only natural that people try to find myths and symbols to explain what they cannot otherwise understand.

If a race is dominant in an area of the world, its myths will be used to justify that dominance and triumph. Thus, in much of American history many whites used the biblical story of the patriarch Noah's cursed son, Ham, to justify Negro slavery—even though the biblical story itself gives no hint that "Hamites" were black. American Indians had creation stories, on the other hand, that told them how to endure and outlast the white intruders. In the 1960s when

minorities became freshly assertive, most of them reached for religious claims and symbols to justify their self-understandings. Therefore the Reverend Albert Cleage spoke of the 'religiocification" of the black movement. Indian Power, Chicano Power, Latino Power—these were slogans that were often accompanied by a recovery of religious rituals and slogans.

Those in the majority can usually see other people's myths but not their own. Thus White Anglo-Saxon Protestants, the WASPS who were once numerically dominant in America (though today WASPs born of native WASP parentage represent only about 30 percent of the population), were convinced that God had created them a superior race and given them a manifest destiny and mission to rule in the world. In the 1890s even the more humane of them felt that their race was normative, that other races would be extirpated, merged. or upgraded into a zone that would make them white in appearance and outlook.

On the basis of these myths and dogmas, people then go about putting practice into their institutional life. To take for the moment but one example: For years Americans have heard the truism that Sunday morning worship time was the most segregated hour of the week. Whites and blacks had less to do with each other that day than any other. They set up educational and housing systems that would institutionalize racism. When they did so, they usually found that religious appeals fortified their activities. The guiltier their conscience or the weaker their case, the more they needed support of religious institutions.

Almost anyone who has claimed prophetic status on the American scene has concentrated in recent years on problems of religious racism. The bloodied veterans of such battles in Christian congregations can speak with eloquence about how other aspects of religion wither in the face of racism. Normally decent people who seem to be reasonable and responsive suddenly lose their whole serenity when race comes into their orbit. The timid ones who have always had "one honest sermon in their drawers," the sermon they would preach if they had courage or opportunity, will usually confide that such a message would concentrate on the racial attitudes of the pious—of any race. (Those who were long discriminated against have, for either reflexive or reflective reasons, replied in kind; most of them are also separationist after two centuries of national life.)

The periscope that is turned out from the ghettos all Americans inhabit shows instantly a vision of limited tolerance, at best, and overt religious racism at worst. One way to begin that survey is to notice that Americans have always used religion to help justify their attempts to exclude the racial groups that have not yet become acceptable. Indians were not willing to be converted; despite the whites' announced intention to carry on mission among them and to serve them, they were cool or they fought back. In a brief time the Christians had an ideology ready. They explained that the devil had taken the Indians captive. At Harvard they seriously debated whether Indians had a soul. Never were Indian religious values appraised seriously.

The Indian was not a person; he could be killed or removed to even more remote reservations. American white Christians almost unanimously concurred in such policies.

American blacks who were brought in for chattel slavery were always regarded as property, not as persons. While whites made some missionary efforts later and helped make provision or room for blacks to worship, it was clear in practice that they had religious doctrines to explain race. Scientific racism was not on the scene until the middle of the nineteenth century. But in a pious society the Bible was easily used to define slavery, to make it legitimate, and to justify efforts to keep blacks without any rights. In fact, Christians led in the development of racist ideologies until late in the nineteenth century. Sometimes they would deny baptism to blacks, because it was believed that blacks would thereby gain personal legal status. While the majorities were insistent on retaining family structures and were against sexual intercourse outside the family, they helped to break up Negro slave families and refused to perform marriage rites which might imply that blacks were legal persons.

The Chinese were needed for mining camps in the West, but when they came in numbers they had to be excluded. Japanese seemed to be more welcome, but weeks after World War II broke out in 1941 they were herded into concentration camps while Hollywood and the churches conspired to portray them as less than fully human. The Statue of Liberty's verse by Emma Lazarus, the one that invited the world's tired, poor,

huddled masses to these shores, was defended only in limited contexts.

Once new peoples were here, the religious majorities did not allow them to see America as a promised land. They were trapped in a land where their sweat was welcomed but they could not publicize their own myths. Little wonder that many blacks have kept alive some dream of Afro-American political reality, where there would be freedom. Jews have welcomed and needed Israel as a land of alternative, to provide identity or meaning and purpose.

The churches conspire to reinforce patterns of racial inequality. While northern churchmen found it easy to demonstrate for legal changes that brought about better circumstances for southern blacks—witness the rise in the numbers of them who hold office in Mississippi or Alabama—they disappeared when the battle for rights came to affect northern urban policies. Most American Christians are at ease in their ignorance of American Indian policy. They demonstrate that they regard people of the southern hemisphere or of Asia more lightly than they do Euro-Americans; and show lack of interest in reports of miseries in the developing nations while they make great human dramas of the struggles of even a few whites.

Religious America has it in its power to bring about legal changes that would better racial minorities. But these policies and possibilities are often shrugged off. Christian America says, "You cannot legislate morality." That may be true; how would one prove or disprove it? But it can be shown that a society can make

legal arrangements in which new moral patterns can emerge—as most white southerners would agree after seeing changes for the better in recent years. (Similarly, changes in real estate laws in the North could help eliminate "blockbusting" and other practices that help rule out the possibility of creative urban change.) Religious America has it in its power to make the difference. The late Dr. Robert Spike, a white leader in matters of race, once argued that if churches got behind efforts to change housing laws and if their own members worked for justice, America could see a change on the Tuesday following the Sunday that the biblical idea caught on.

A special problem of religion in the field of race has to do with hypocrisy. Christians, for example, share so many of the values of their nonreligious neighbors that one may not always expect heroism from them. But what is nagging from a biblically prophetic point of view is the ability the believers of all races have to justify their chosen ways by reference to religious claims. "God wills" that we live the way we do. Instead of using the spiritual accent as a basis for repentance, it often appears to support backlashing or the stiffening of resistance.

Americans have been understandably contented with their racial policies. These have produced "the good life." The Indians' land was expropriated, to the benefit of the conqueror. The blacks in their slavery made the plantation policy work, so that the South could be economically productive. After that system was no longer feasible, according to Professor Eugene Geno-

vese and numerous other students of the slave system, southern leadership helped perpetuate the slavery in order to keep a "way of life" intact. A cleric was always at hand to show that God had so willed it.

In contemporary America, despite some progress in selected areas, race remains the blight on the conscience. It is taken for granted as a kind of fated, dooming problem; citizens greet it with a sense of inevitability. A British newsman several summers ago casually put to me a question as we strolled from lunch on Michigan Avenue in Chicago: "Tell me, if a black family were to move into ————" (and he named a nearby suburb), "What would happen?" I said, not dropping a beat, "The house would be bombed and the family would, if it resisted, be killed." Later I read the report of the newsman's tour. He said he asked ten Chicagoans the same question in the same way, and all ten—without a sense of shock or outrage or even without a pause—had given the answer I did. The community he mentioned is one of the most "churched" in the metropolitan area since religious organizations serve as the center of most people's lives. Yet it would not occur to them that bombing or killing a member of another race in order to preserve an equity might be an act that should come under judgment. (Let me add parenthetically that the people of that community are not wholly wrong in their vision. The way matters are arranged in the urban north it is true that letting the first black in would mean, in little time at all, a complete and fiscally devastating community change. Before one judges these urban victims, backed up to the

edge of the ghetto in ethnic enclaves, it is important to examine the systemic circumstance that makes their response so tragically inevitable.)

The barriers of religiously justified racism remain. How many Gentiles know Jews well? Who in the majority knows even one Indian? How many white churches have black members, or vice versa? The percentages are so low that they represent virtual insignificance on a national scale. What is worse, the trend is away from what little measure of interaction had been known some years ago.

If in any element of national life Americans carry the burden of a past it is in the issue of race. One has the impression that if we were "starting from scratch" today, everything would be different. Had whites to deal today with the Indians they first encountered: free, self-determining, talented, brave—it is hard to picture them coming up with such negative imagery as that which they have developed after 350 years of exploitation. Today's Indian is demoralized, often apparently leaderless; there is little opportunity for the tribes to come together in coalitions of spokesmen. Instead, interest groups fight each other, at the expense of Indians.

One would like to think that today's religious whites would not enslave blacks even if it were possible, feasible, or economically virtually necessary—as it appeared in late colonial times up to the War between the States. If only blacks had been free to immigrate as did northern hemispheric people, America's religious believers could, one supposes, look at them and cope

with them in different ways. Yet a glance at the larger society suggests that problems would still remain. Race is tied in to so many other psychological, social, and economic issues that it may serve as little more than a way of measuring what else is wrong with America.

People who are internally secure, who have and know an identity, who are free to assert themselves, have less need to use another people as a floor for their own self-esteem. It is the insecure, the embattled, those who are unsure of who they are or what they are here for, who are forced to find ideologies that justify racism. And they are also often the people forced by circumstance to live next to the problem, to have to deal with it most urgently. To date the people who would use Christian or similar norms to work for reconciliation have not been sufficiently in touch with the problems and needs of the insecure. Therefore "liberal" efforts at improving situations are exposed as superficial or hypocritical by Middle America, and the progressives themselves find one more group against whom to express their own refined styles of prejudice. On many issues of social justice prophets become programmers, offering solutions. On this one, they weep.

-7-

Enduring Clericalism

THROUGH the ages there has been a danger that religious leadership has dominated over the followers or that the followers have tended to permit leaders to take on the whole burden of spiritual expression. In the Western world this disease is called clericalism, after the word "cleric," a characteristic form of leadership in that world. When people are critical of clericalism, they are not pointing to the obvious fact that complex movements need leaders. Nor is there anything especially wrong with endowing those leaders by means of special sanctions. They may be ordained, somewhat set apart sacramentally or by some other sign or token. Such sanctions may be necessary if leaders are to assert themselves at all, and to carry out their responsibilities.

Clericalism refers instead to the formation of a caste or elite of people who take or who are granted powers to control society or the lives of people in it. They create a world of self-importance, as if everything that mattered had to do with the clergy. They demand special favors and honors and develop sys-

tems of ideas that make followers and laity into second-class citizens. They cultivate the impression that they are especially holy and that their holiness serves to make others holy or that others are inferior.

Such clericalism takes a different form in a free society than it did when religion was formally established by law. In historic establishmentarian cultures, the clergy officially shared in ruling. The lines between what we call church and state today were drawn less sharply. The pope had powers that emperors might envy; he could excommunicate peoples or put them under an interdict. The terms of such an arrangement meant that no one in a legal territory or kingdom could receive the sacraments and, hence, eternal life. Such clericalism was a potent political weapon. The clerics were turned to for answers in philosophy and science; they laid down all the moral rules.

The Protestant Reformation may have meant the end of interdicts, but not necessarily of clericalism. In Calvin's Geneva as well as in most other "mainstream" segments of the Reformation, the clergy retained enormous power over people's lives. But the moment had come when a new sense of the laity might have emerged. Theologian Hendrik Kraemer in *A Theology of the Laity* pointed out why the laity did not develop on schedule. In part this resulted from an identity crisis in the clergy. While few Protestants claimed that ordination was a sacrament, they kept on ordaining people to be ministers. But they were not sure just what this meant. So they devised functional lines for the determination of the clergy. To be a clergyman

meant that one had studied theology and biblical writings in a special way at a special place. It meant that an ecclesiastical body had approved this training and licensed the person; then a congregation or other jurisdiction would call him—and even the "him" was important. The distinction was often intellectual. The clergyman was supposed to be a better trained and hence better expositor of the Scriptures.

This meant in most Protestant groups the laity were inevitably if partly accidentally relegated to second class status. They were the Christians, members of the priesthood of all believers, who could not do certain things. Most of all, they could not preach or administer the sacraments. Not to preach left them confused about their witness and responsibilities. The Protestant laity was therefore often as passive, submissive, and uncreative as the Catholic laity had been. While what is sometimes called the "left-wing" of Protestantism was a bit more free and open about lay freedom, including freedom to preach, this wing either had also made compromises with clericalism or it was underrepresented in the America that became a nation two centuries ago.

Today clericalism lives on, for natural and artificial reasons alike. For example, in a complex society it is natural for most men and women of the religious groups to be preoccupied with their daily work and not free to concentrate on many details of religious organizational life. The minister or rabbi may be one of the few well-equipped believers to be "on the scene" when many important decisions are made. He may,

for example, turn out to be a one-person building committee or construction advisory crew when a new church or synagogue is built, simply because his clientele is otherwise preoccupied while the builders are on the scene. So he is consulted and he assumes the role.

Again, in a technical society, what is everyone's job is no one's job. So people assign to the cleric an astonishing range of duties, all focused in some concept of ministry. Sometimes laity simply abdicate responsibilities, because they are lazy or they are tired of fighting the minister who preempts all the attractive spots. They may withdraw because they live in a money world, and they reason that the minister is getting the money for serving. They may only half-believe in what the religious group stands for. They may simply be turned off by clerical preening. Whatever the reasons, we are left with a bad dose of clericalism. Not many ministers will say that they want the world to be arranged this way, and many of them would genuinely escape it, but somehow the system persists.

A periscope directed to those who adhere to religious groups finds clericalism on all sides. This is readily visible in the double-standard implied whenever laity expect clergy to be substitute holy men for them. They like to be free to flirt with the edges of their churches' moral standards, but feel uneasy if the minister does. Thus in many Protestant churches, where there is an ethos or prohibition against drinking alcoholic beverages, they will secretly indulge—or even openly partake out of sight of the clergy. But if the clergy share their way of life, they are shocked. They expect minis-

ters to speak in hushed and hollow tones, not to reveal the true range of human emotions, to be soft and compromising or unprincipled adapters to what their congregations want them to be. Perhaps on these terms the minister, priest, or rabbi will generate a kind of holiness that will rub off on them.

Conversely, some ministers cultivate the image. They adopt a "chancel tone" and talk in false and artificial tones. They make productions out of the simplest human gestures. The language of piety afflicts everything that they do, including the telling of time. They expect discounts and other privileges that often compromise both the professionalism and Christian commitment that go with the office. These are very broad and sweeping charges, and have little to do with the lives of tens of thousands of faithful men and women in ministry. They should not be applied to everyone indiscriminately. Instead they describe a cultural stereotype that is easily checked out through observation. If one minister may not fit the "clericalist" image, he or she can easily point to others who do. (Do not ask them to point; judging and gossip about this will not necessarily decrease clericalism, but it may well increase clerical backbiting.)

One vivid example of lay passivity in the face of clericalism is the general absence of lay people in the circles out of which the theological interpretation of life occurs. Almost all church theology is clerical; almost always ordained ministers in seminaries or in congregations are called upon to depict the meaning of the Christian life in any profound way. This is un-

fortunate, since the clergy have a partial and somehow distorted picture of the church in the world. Recently this has begun to change, especially during the past couple decades as more and more men and women who teach in secular colleges and universities come up through and remain in lay ranks. But it must also be said that most of their religious specialties tend to be outside the range of the language of believing communities. They tend to be specialists in non-Western religions, or religious history, or religion in literature. Church theology remains clericalized. If this is a problem in Protestantism it is especially acute in Catholicism. Yet there is nothing that says theology in Catholicism has to be written and done by clerics. Modern European Roman Catholic churches have seen much creative enterprise by notable laymen.

On another level, the local church is often clerically dominated. What the priest says, goes. Sometimes there are many motions that suggest that the laity have a part, but basic decisions pass them by and they chiefly are asked to be supportive of programs that have been decided for them.

On the national scene, when people ask, "What does the church say?" they really mean, "What does the clergy say?" The lobbies, the celebrities, the public relations people all tend to be made up of clerics or people with clerical mentalities. For that reason, despite all the competences that show up, the whole range of religious followers' initiatives and perspectives are not as free to appear. In many sociological or church renewal studies it appears that even progressive minis-

ters often seem threatened by truly competent and assertive laity, and draw back from making room for them. Denominational periodicals often tend to be highly clericalized. It is natural that clergy would receive disproportionate attention, since they do represent larger groups and it is hard for readers to locate everyone who is untitled. But very often these periodicals create a false world inside real ones, a clergyperson's view of what is good or bad, important or unimportant.

Americans come by their clericalism quite naturally. Some of the problem arises from an American virtue, if it can be called that. By this I mean to point to the general absence to date of a tradition of anticlericalism. In many European nations the minister is a derided figure and the clergy as a bloc is often portrayed as representing its own interests against the people's. In America because of the variety of religions represented it is harder to have a bloc or to speak of ministerial stereotypes. Therefore there has been less motivation to break through American clericalism.

Clericalism takes its root from the earliest settlements, back to the days when Roman Catholic missionaries, both secular and religious clergy—which means those set aside to be exposed to the world and those set aside to be withdrawn a bit in monastic orders —set the terms for work among the Indians. In Virginia and other southern Anglican colonies the clergy were a less formal and formidable group, but they asserted their privileges. But it was in New England where a very gifted and potent set of clerics estab-

lished themselves as standing above the community, there to serve as moral arbiters and judges. There the cleric assumed almost a law-giving and law-enforcing role that later generations took to naturally.

In the scheme of things in the majority faiths of America there is no special good reason for setting the minister above the flock this way, but the pattern became established. One would have thought that on the rough and tumble of the frontier clericalism would have disappeared. But there people hungered for a kind of order, and even the most ill-equipped and illiterate itinerant who wanted to hang out his shingle as a "Reverend" was expected to be accorded special respect. And these backwoods preachers no less than the "downy, sapient D.D.s," as one of them called the more urbane and pretentious ministers—took care to see to their prerogatives and privileges.

In this particular instance our own pattern of observation can be broken in the case of the national founding fathers, who throughout this book have been regarded as a kind of spiritual leadership. It must be said in fairness to them that they were largely a lay movement, not overly mindful of clerical privilege. Still, even in their circles a breed of Unitarian ministers established themselves as a kind of priestly class that did not look much different than the older Calvinist conservatives.

In the nineteenth century the laity almost broke through again and again. Thus early in the period in a network of humanitarian and evangelical organizations the laity played a big part. But as years passed

there was a kind of subtle drift from the lay-centered, interdenominational character of these boards to a more formal clericalized and denominational set of bureaucrats. Women in particular were kept from fulfilling themselves in these activities. Before long lay people were reconfined to second-echelon activities. The dirty work, that which was not decisive, could be assigned the laity. But what really mattered in these organizations was again in the hands of "the reverends."

One would have thought that at several thousand miles removed from Rome and in the new American conditions, Roman Catholicism could have broken from its old clericalist patterns. Some efforts were made in the form of a movement devoted to "lay trusteeism." In this pattern church properties—then as now largely in the names and hands of the clerics and especially the hierarchy—would have been in the hands of lay trustees. Here and there the pattern began to show signs of succeeding. But it seemed to be too radical for Catholic polity and before long the policy was dropped—even though here and there there were minor schisms over it. For well over a century the Catholic laity lapsed into submissiveness. Abilities to lead were atrophied. When after the Second Vatican Council in the 1960s there was encouragement for a more lay-run church, few had interest or abilities. Many of them soon became frustrated and tired and left the scene. Others became token lay representatives in a world where basic decisions were left to the clergy.

The case of Judaism is even more striking. In Eu-

rope the rabbi is a lay person, a teacher without "sacramental" or pastoral duties. But in America, whether to fill out the "three-faith" picture alongside minister and priest or because the clericalizing impulse has been so strong, the rabbi has to take on strange new clerical roles, often at the expense of lay status.

The twentieth century has seen a great growth in the literacy and competence of the laity. Whereas once upon a time a rabbi, priest, or minister would be not only the most educated but often the only educated person in a community, what he said mattered more. But today's professional constantly confronts people who are more gifted than he at most aspects of religious life. Some progress has been made. But old attitudes are hard to break down, and in far too many instances the real or important world, as reflected in congregations and religious periodicals and community attitudes, is still closed within a clerical circle. Ministers complain about the circle, but do not always find or do not sometimes want to find ways to see it broken open.

-8-

Male-Dominated Religion and Society

A SOCIETY can be judged by the way it treats its least fortunate citizens. If this statement is true, then it ought to be at least as true that a religion can be judged by the way it regards the majority of its members. If they exist only for the sake of the leaders, of an elite minority, something must be wrong with the whole. On those terms it can be shown that quite consistently through the centuries American religion or the religions of America have mistreated their majorities. It happens that slightly over half of the population is made up of women. So far as can be known, women have conventionally made up an even slightly higher percentage of the church-going population. How have they been treated?

If one were to consult the history books, only one conclusion can emerge. They are at best neglected. Scan the indices of even the best of these, and you will find very few women's names. Is this the fault of the

historians? In a way, perhaps, yes. They could go beyond conventional sources and find women wherever they have been in the American religious past. However, the fault may lie even more in the sources and documents on which chroniclers and storytellers depend. These consist of records of church meetings, clerical gatherings, and denominational conventions. There decisions are made that affect the whole religious enterprise.

Through most of the years in most of such gatherings women have been almost entirely absent. Whoever goes no further than the records of these public events and affairs will have little to write about, so far as women are concerned. A closer reading will show, however, that women are discussed in their absence. Now and then the subject of women's place and status comes up. Then the attitudes vary from condescension to degradation. That is, the male clerics and other leaders will assign women cozy and comfortable but essentially powerless roles, allegedly out of respect for the "fair sex" status. Or they will draw on the history of religion or on various philosophical and theological categories to go so far as to justify a second-class citizenship for the women.

Those who are trying today to make changes and to help people "raise consciousness" usually take one of two tacks. They can show that there is basically no tradition to which people can appeal in their interest in having religion serve as an instrument for women's liberation. So few religions or spiritual movements of the past have much to offer. On those terms, the

Bible's "patriarchalism" is no exception. It grew out of a male-dominated world and reflects attitudes that would enslave women or yield little to them.

The other approach rereads the past and sees that at least the root or germ of a better situation is implied. Thus in Paul's letter to the Galatians, even that notorious dismisser of women showed that "in Christ" there is "neither male nor female." Now and then in Christian history women have asserted themselves, and their recall is important in a history of liberation. The same is less true in Jewish history, but there are moments on which to reflect and from which to draw. In this reading, when modernity came and people wanted to live out of the logic of biblical themes—as they did when they abolished slavery even though biblical authors lived with it—they betrayed the logic of this history. They failed to permit a development of religious life. Male attitudes went further than inherited theology did to keep women down.

Most of the anthologies of women's liberation have no difficulty finding anti-women texts in the religious past. One of the most cited prayers is a Jewish prayer that thanks God for not having created the congregation as heathens or slaves. Then the men say: "Blessed are you, Lord our God, King of eternity, who has not created me a woman." And the women say: "Blessed are you, Lord our God, King of eternity, who has created me in accord with His will." Some rabbis say that men are simply thanking God for having spared them women's hard lot, but the connection of women with heathens and slaves is obvious.

The situation today does not seem to be much different. On the surface, of course, there is a great involvement on the part of women. The observer who looks in on the worshiping congregation of almost any American religious body, is likely to find more women than men present. The organizational chart of Jewish or Christian congregations or of almost any religious movement will find whole categories of Ladies Aids and Women's Auxiliaries. But that is precisely the problem. To be in an auxiliary suggests that the real action is elsewhere and a group of people with talent is excluded from the decisive sphere. They can give of their time and talents and money in support of what someone else—namely, the males—determine as policy.

Sometimes it is argued that the situation is changing. It would be hard to imagine that religion could successfully stand apart from the achievements in both consciousness-raising and new opportunities for expression. But it is not pioneering; there seems to be a kind of reluctant "going along" and grudging assent to the new women's situation, often coupled by some sexist attempts at humor on the part of place-yielding males who yield no more than is necessary at any particular moment.

Ordination represents a test case. Most churches are not sure of what they mean by ordination; only Roman Catholics and a few "high church" Protestants assign it a sacramental status. Yet almost everybody has a rite through which people who are qualified or called become members of a set-aside clergy. Usually

some sort of special prayers go with the rite, and special privileges and sanctions are to follow.

Most Protestant denominations now ordain women, though some multimillion member groups do not and, of course, Roman Catholics exclude women from full clerical status. Without such status, women cannot really enter into the inner spheres of decision-making. Not to be ordained has become a legitimate symbol of second-class citizenship also for that huge majority of women who make no effort to be qualified and accepted as clerics. But what is more important than actual exclusion is the set of barriers that often remain after they are ordained. Few of them become heads of congregations of their own. They are directors of education, ministers of music, assistant pastors, campus workers. These are all honorable enough professions. But if they are restricted to these spheres, they are hardly fully free. Very often women enter certain professional ranks and castes more on the principle of tokenism ("We ought to have two or three women on this seminary faculty of forty, don't you think?") than on simple merit or on the principles of representationality.

The attitudes toward ordination include many reflections of culture and habit. They usually are not exclusively theological, and one often has the impression that those who keep women away from leadership roles do not even use all the liberating theology available to them. The clergy has been all male for so long and the lay leadership has been dominated by men for so many

centuries that people do not know how to think differently about the subject.

Theological problems often do lie at the root of these practices, however. This is certainly the case for Judaism, whose holy books are full of remarks about the special taint of women, especially in connection with their menstruation and childbearing. Orthodox synagogues still engage in sex-segregation. Black Muslim religion, one of the more thriving black emphases of recent decades, preserves from orthodox Islam, of which it is not a true part, the strictures against women achieving high status. And Christianity has in its primal documents a number of passages to which people can appeal when they try to segregate and demean women.

The villain in much of this is St. Paul, author of New Testament letters that reflect so much of life in the early church. His point of view was based in his reading of the Hebrew Scriptures and in some mysterious sources in his own make-up and outlook. Women were created out of men, and were to be subordinate to them. For that reason in one passage he says that women are "to keep silence in the church." (Few notice that a few inches of Scripture text away from this passage is another that says *when* women prophesy and pray they are to keep their heads covered.) It takes no great skill to perceive that few Christians follow Paul literally in all his other opinions—for example, about haircuts and veils over heads. But here the prejudices and habits of males are most cherished and on this subject Paul is followed literally.

Advocates of women's liberation in the churches have enemies other than men to contend with. In sexual matters as in their racial counterparts there are the female equivalents of "Uncle Toms." These aunts are women who have been so conditioned to submit to male dominance and to accept uncritically readings of ancient Scriptures that reflect these views that they do not speak up for themselves. They continue to elect and appoint men as their leaders. They are often critical of and embarrassed about the more aggressive attempts to find new places for women in religious professions and decision-making. Far from proving that males are not at fault, it only reinforces the picture of their past effectiveness at having their way, even in fashioning images and determining rules for women.

At bicentennial time people naturally look backward for help. In the connections between women and religion there is not much of a past to look to for help. Colonial religion represents a rather consistent disaster area. The sermons that have been passed down to us are almost unanimous in their assumption that women belong in the home. Women, we must assume, largely accepted this picture, since few of them found escape from such constriction. Higher education was ruled out; how so many of them became so literate remains a wonder. Certainly it was not the Harvards or the Yales that made room for them.

Elementary education was to become a zone wherein women could excel in the nineteenth century. Ruth Miller Elson's *Guardians of Tradition* scans the school textbooks of the century and finds many of them writ-

ten by women. But most of these were daughters of parsonages, people who knew their place even as they were looking for new ones. Their attitudes toward religion and toward women's expression largely mirror those derived from their often moderately conservative fathers, so far as this subject is concerned. When the Sunday School movement began to be acceptable in early United States history, it was often opposed by ministers not simply because it was new or was a threat to established ways of doing things but because it was often in the hands of women.

No colony shows a bright picture; the New England examples are often the worst. The few women who did speak up usually had such radical visions for the future or such angry perspectives on the present that they could easily be typed as heretics and banished. The case of Anne Hutchinson is perhaps the best example; men who shared her views were also banished, but the records of her exiling show special uncomprehension on the part of the orthodox and special venom about her womanly status. The best known women in colonial religion were these heretics or, unfortunately, the unfortunate witches of Salem.

If the "religion of the republic" that derives from the founders of the nation is often a liberating option alongside the more binding biblical traditions, in the case of women in religion these founding fathers— whoever heard of our nation's founding mothers?— are an exception. They were supposed to have been enlightened, to have been alert to new stirrings in philosophy and nature. They read European books and

wanted to be regarded as inhabitants of a kind of future. They would put together a new world. But to them women remained chiefly decorative accessories or objects.

These fathers were essentially political, not religious figures. And women at that time were not in legislative assemblies and did not even have a vote. So they could have virtually no political power. The Abigail Adamses and the Dolly Madisons parlayed their talents into a place in history, and are not forgotten in the textbook tradition. But their direct influence on events was small. If that was the case in politics, it was even more so in religion. We do have some accounts of prominent clerical wives; Sarah Pierrepont Edwards is the best example. We see them beginning with wills of their own; in their diaries they often record how grudging their own assent to male worlds was. But in the end they accepted their place and helped contribute to the myths of female inferiority and to patriarchalism in religion.

The nineteenth century saw many religious revivals and awakenings. But all the revivalists and almost all the preachers were male. Women were eventually allowed to give to, organize for, support, and finally represent the foreign missions of the church. They would not poison or confuse "the heathen." But acceptance at home was longer and slower in coming.

In that century as in colonial times, the women who were expressive were often forced to work outside the usual channels and many of them were heretical in the eyes of the main line religious leaders. Many of the

founders of new faiths were women. Mary Baker Eddy founded Christian Science. Ellen White picked up the pieces of William Miller's design and gave essential shape to Seventh Day Adventism. The Fox sisters of western New York heard spirit-rapping and originated a new Spiritualism. Anne Besant introduced some kinds of Eastern and occult religion under the name of Theosophy. Their orthodox counterparts did not find a place.

When the feminist movements and the agitations for women's suffrage appeared on the scene, these often had to appear over against religion. Many of the gifted leaders of women's movements derived from evangelicalism, but they had to turn anticlerical and sometimes even antireligious. They were frustrated countless times in their efforts to link up with libertarians and liberals in religion. When the earlier stages of the feminist movement collapsed in the twentieth century, many churchmen rejoiced. Ever since, the liberation of women has been uphill in the areas or spheres in which America's historic religions have had much influence.

Part III
The American Experience

-9-

The Self-Seekers in Religion

THE SAME religion that can expect much of people can offer much to them. And while religion has it in its genius to offer abundant life and, often, eternal happiness, it can often be perverted beyond recognition by people who forget its demands and turn only to its promises. The German theologian who lost his life at the end of World War II to Nazis in a concentration camp, Dietrich Bonhoeffer, liked to speak about "cheap grace." People accepted what religion offered without accepting its disciplines. As a poet parodied it: "I like to commit sins, God likes to forgive them; the world is admirably arranged."

Sometimes the case never even reaches the point where sin and forgiveness enter the discussion. At such times religion is uprooted from context and turned into a device for offering everything to self seekers. In the 1970s many in the black community have been embarrassed by an evangelist of "green power," the Rev-

erend Ike Eikerenkoetter, who draws funds from the urban aspirant poor and promises them that they will get rich. He is nothing more than an overt, extravagant, and flamboyant successor to several centuries' worth of religious leaders who promised everything in the name of religion.

Religion holds special potency for people who would like to use it for success. It is mysterious, and hints at mysterious arrangements with the gods. If only one can find the key to the proper relationship with deity, certainly fates will be kind, and only good will happen to me. I was not put into the world just for suffering and failure, while others prosper materially and become popular. I must learn the proper rites and formulae by which to appease the powers outside me and to develop the powers within me.

On such grounds, America has seen countless "positive thinking" movements. Many of them at least pay lip service to orthodoxy, so that some of the basic teachings of a religious tradition survive. But these are recast in contexts that leave the original vision almost unrecognizable and certainly unrecognized. At heart they are all examples of "cheap grace."

The world has long been full of such movements, but for a variety of reasons America has been especially rich in its hospitality toward them. Why? In fairness let it first be said that some people propagate these views because they honestly believe them. Religion has worked for them. They led aimless and unproductive lives. After a conversion and through various disciplines they came to a new way of life. They

want to pass the secret on to others, often unmindful of the inability others might have to begin on the same bottom rungs of the same ladders they have used. They are simply evangelists.

Others, however, become hucksters and hypesters. American religion is a competitive venture. Whoever wishes to, can set up shop and make any kind of claims he or she would like. In such a market, the more extravagant claims, the better. People take note of the weirder promises, some of which have worked for someone somewhere. (Everyone knows a cousin or friend who had his vacation paid for by Lady Luck at Las Vegas; it *has* to happen to me! This approach discounts the fact that the next ninety-nine people lost their bankrolls at the same gambling tables.)

Whoever listens to the dreary jangle of Sunday morning religious radio soon notes that no one is getting rich by demanding sacrifice—beyond the dollar or two of sacrifice that are solicited by the speaker. They gain their followings by offering the positive benefits of religion. Such people plant their churches in fashionable suburbs where people of bad conscience about their wealth seek good conscience about their wealth. There prosperous "way of life" religions seem to be offered to those who have not yet made it.

The offers are of various kinds. Not a few are as full of the promise of material substance as are Reverend Ike's. The appeals and claims are not always so overt. It is not simply that one uses the blessed prayer cloth or gives lucky money and blessings and luck arrive. Rather, there is a personality change. One be-

comes better liked, more positive in outlook; people have confidence and invest in the new believer. All is well.

Sometimes instead of material substance only the attitude that produces it is advertised. Just as often physical health is the promise. While most religions, including of course biblical faith, make much of the divine aspects of healing, the religion of self-seeking makes an absolute out of physical health. While in the Bible God comes to the sick, in these cults illness is seen as a moral flaw just as poverty is seen as the result of vice by impatient and successful positive thinkers. Sometimes in place of the material, the attitudinal, or the physically health-supplying promises, religious experiences as ends in themselves make up the "more abundant life" of the religious peddler's offerings.

When religion is exploited for such purposes it is most easy to add up all the alternatives and to package what might be called the "religion of the American way of life." Such a religion exists in church and state, in religious organizations, and in the claims of national existence. It attracts energies of people in the churches and it sometimes attracts energies from them.

Wherever one looks, the religion of American self-seeking presents itself. The system begins with little children, in a world of reward and promise. The effort is made to put them into a groove from the beginning. There they are not to question the national way of life nor to admire heroes who question it. Instead they are to become docile and sheeplike, following in the way of people who have been most successful and conforming.

The home is touted as the place where these influences can best be nurtured. Anything which assaults the conventional middle class family structure has to be defined as alien to the spirit of true religion.

The prospering youth movements in religion are those that panoply the most beauty queens and athletic heroes, the well-endowed and self-made people who improve their endowments and make more of themselves. In such advertised religion one almost always loses any sense of identification with or empathy for the abject poor. Most of the people of the world can never come to the point where aspiration means much. Many children of the ghetto have no opportunity to improve themselves at all; far from being better understood as a result of religious teaching, they are even more despised.

In the adult world the successful religious organizations are advertised for the successes they produce. The moral pattern they develop sanctions the approved standards of the community but allows for hypocrisy. The moral preachment there rarely attacks the kind of ethical flaws built into their system; executive cheating or rounding corners on income tax would seldom be mentioned. Instead, the people are congratulated for the ways they lifted themselves by their bootstraps and won Brownie points.

As far as the social sphere is concerned, Americans regularly show that they do not want their religious institutions to be ethical. Charles Y. Glock and Rodney Stark, after they made their surveys, came to the conclusion that ethics would be the end of institutional

religion. Dean Kelley studied *Why Conservative Churches Are Growing* (or why liberal ones were not growing) and came up with a result that can easily be translated into the idea that religious people wanted the world to remain as they had inherited it or put it together. They did not want ethical concerns having to do with the larger society propagated among them, though, in fairness, it must be said that the strict ones were often quite ready to undertake personal and private disciplines for their faith.

Religion comes to be supportive of class distinctions and to congratulate those who have prospered. Behind these values there stand several centuries of temptations for American religionists to offer rather than demand or to call for adaptation to a way of life that is rather than to a judgment upon it and a going beyond it.

The roots for the tendency may be as old as human nature. It is always comforting to have a cozy arrangement with the gods. But our story properly begins with the people who came to the American shores. The Spaniards and the Portuguese here set a pace in their thirst for gold. They used all the trappings and symbols of religion to fulfill their purposes, but they saw their efforts best crowned when their religion paid off most.

More familiar to many Americans is the arrangement worked out with God by the Puritans in New England. They came in the name of a God who was far beyond human manipulation. But they could hardly be expected to serve one whose ways and promises could

not be known at all. So they had already adapted their grasp of him. The adaptation may have been a genuine religious vision; at our place in history there is no valid reason for doubting its authenticity or sincerity. Nor is it out of line with a way of reading Christian revelation.

The key move, however, had drastic results. In the words of Perry Miller, they began to "chain" God. He had to be able to be counted upon. If he were absolutely inscrutable, he could not be. His ways could be known. And they offered prosperity to those who would serve him well. For decades such a view did little to corrupt the colonies. But they eventually moved from "Puritan to Yankee" as they saw their mercantile ventures produce prosperity. Obviously, God was telling his people that they were good. He was certainly letting them know that their investments were proper and their means Christian. They now had the right to get better and better at what they set out to do. Religion need no longer haunt or trouble them; now it should lead them to prosperity and progress.

The scholar Max Weber ventured a controversial generalization when he called the new way of life the "Protestant Ethic." He noted the concurrent rise of capitalism plus a kind of Calvinism, and argued a cause-and-effect relation between the two. The thesis claims too much and is easily misused. There has been capitalism without Calvinism; it was being shaped in fifteenth-century Venice far from any place where the earnest French-Swiss and Germans ever invested or prayed. And there have been Calvinisms that were not

particularly conducive to capitalism and material prosperity. Still, more than coincidence was at stake in the rise of northwest European and Anglo-American religious interpretations of the day's work, worth, and material prosperity. And these came together in especially productive ways in the American colonies. In New York the Dutch burghers may not have wanted a pastor in sight, but they developed a religion of self-seeking as much as did New Englanders or the more casual Virginia planters. Little wonder that many religions of oppressed people in America have picked up the idea that godliness leads to riches.

The other religion that becomes so visible at bicentennial times, the founding fathers' faith, was also devoted to what Saint-Just called a new idea, the idea of "happiness." The heavenly city of the eighteenth-century philosophers had its worldly obsessions. One might be personally frugal and self-disciplined, as a Benjamin Franklin might be. But he was sure that the religiously good life had to be productive of human material good.

The nineteenth century saw the fulfillment of countless religions of positive thinking. It is possible to note the transitions if one compares an older generation of evangelical clerics with their sons, or senior philanthropists with their juniors. In the older generation there were still some restraints against tying religion to material self-seeking. There is no reason here to go into detail on the kind of obvious criticisms that could be raised against the older static view. It was out of date, based on some misreadings of Scripture and his-

tory, nonfunctional for the new situation of frontier and factory.

The older view, however, still had in it room for a "theology of failure." It helped people account for and live with the rough tosses of the dice called destiny. In theological terms, it still picked up the biblical love of the poor and the suffering. This view reckoned with the lures and hazards of wealth, health, and prosperity. The rich man could hardly be part of the kingdom. Only with God would that be possible. The rich should regard their riches as temptations and risks. The poor, on the other hand, were to be content with their status. God had placed them there. They might improve their place, but if they did not they were not to become envious or grabby.

Such a view might be paralyzing and demeaning, but it had in it some safeguards against the new corollaries of later religious thought. By the late nineteenth century new clerics were using their fathers' signals and symbols about heaven and hell, God and Christ, to support a whole new approach. Now Godliness is in league with riches and all poverty is born of vice; the poor are poor because they deserve to be poor. They have not believed enough or cared enough or improved themselves enough.

In such a climate a large number of "this-worldly" religions of positive thinking began to emerge. Foreign visitors throughout the century remarked on the close alliance of American ministers and bankers, church buildings and banks. They saw dollar signs where crosses or other religious symbols had been. In place of

ethical self-sacrifice they saw people zealous to improve their place and to make the claim that God was doing it through them. By the mid-twentieth century there were few checks against such thinking. A speculator could simply drill a hole in his backyard and become a millionaire from the oil that gushed up. Clearly God was blessing his risks and his labor. Just as clearly, God was edging away the poor and the members of minority groups who in their indolence let the kingdom pass by. In countless gestures, subtle hints, and numerous less-than-subtle-preachments the message has gotten across: God loves those who think positively and seek first the things of this world.

- 10 -

Experience without Interpretation

"THOU SHALT love the Lord thy God with all thy heart, and with all thy soul, and with all thy mind." For a nation as devoted as America claims to have been to the motifs of biblical religion, there has been a curious imbalance in the way the First Commandment has been followed. The people have put a high premium on loving God with heart and soul. They may fail in their fulfillment of that law, but at least they give lip service to following it. However the third part of the injunction, loving God with the mind, has been more limited both in fulfillment and in intention.

Loving God with the mind may mean many different things in different times and places. When it was spoken to the ancient Hebrews and preserved in their literature, very little of what people today picture as intellectual endeavor may have been assumed. The Ten Commandments can hardly be used as a charter for building libraries, inspiring foundations to grant

money for religious research, or providing agendas for organizational activities. In different eras people have conceived of the mind itself in various ways, and it would be a foolish anachronism to take present-day concerns backward into the world of the Bible.

Whenever people wholly neglect the dimensions of mind, however, religion becomes partial and incomplete. Mind religion without heart and soul (or hand) is equally incomplete, but at the moment we are assuming some premium in the American context on such accents while isolating the problem of intellectuality and reason. There has been a fairly consistent suspicion of the use of reason. Somehow the believers have acted as if reason wars on faith and religious practice. They did not invent the fear out of whole cloth; reasons for it are evident. The Bible scorns a kind of human philosophy that leads to a prideful overlooking of the humble and simple weaknesses of God in Christ as grasped in children's faith. The early Christians knew that reason could war against faith. In the modern centuries with the rise of science and industry, secular philosophy and history, people were often asked to choose between the ways of faith and reason, between experience and formulation. Many in the sphere of reason turned "rationalist" and ruled out revelation or the heart's religion.

Misuse of reason in religion is hardly a good excuse for believers to neglect its proper use; the liveliness of experience is no good alternative, if taken exclusively, for religion-of-the-whole that deals with all that people are, including interpreting and formulating beings.

On all these terms, American religion has all too often been deficient.

Those who make so much of experiences such as conversion or enlightenment and play down all attempts to connect these to ways of life or ways of looking at the world overlook too much of biblical revelation. (We are here making reference chiefly to Christianity, because for most of American history other religious forces have not been on the scene in sufficient numbers to permit the making of generalizations at all.) Thus while the New Testament makes clear that an experience of Jesus Christ is vital, its authors never leave the converted persons alone in the decisive "moment before God." They always come down from mountains of transfiguration back to the human city with its problems and posers.

When the anti-intellectual American Christian criticizes anyone who wants to see what the faith has to do with philosophy, politics, or other human enterprises, he overlooks the kind of material presented in the first chapter of Paul's letter to the Colossians. There Jesus Christ is described as the one for whom and in whom and through whom all things are created and in whom "all things hold together." Similar views are presented in the opening chapters of the Fourth Gospel and the Letter to the Ephesians. And Paul's writings throughout are not only impassioned and even burning documents of heart and soul religion; they are also learned theological treatises, addressed to the mind.

American mistrust of intellectuality and interpreta-

tion was born of legitimate causes. For one thing, in the New World the believers had new things on their mind. They were weary about the old dogmatic debates. They had a wilderness to conquer and cities and churches to build. They knew that people could be tied in knots over matters of theology. Sometimes not thinking, keeping things routine, can promote necessary action. The centipede who always ran well but who, when asked how he kept his legs apart ended up thinking about this and getting them tangled, serves as fair warning to the overreflective overinterpreters. The earlier Americans needed wagons and axes and had no space or leisure or skill for the proper use of libraries, wherein much theological lore was reposed. The circuit rider had room only for his personal belongings, a Bible, and a hymnal or prayer book. When there were seminaries, they often did well to import books that formulated and reflected on the faith.

Far from being discontented or apologetic about this situation and far from waiting for its emergency character to end, many North American members of religious organizations and believers in their creeds actually made a virtue out of this necessity. They enshrined their attitude toward the mind. They put a premium on despising theology. Richard Hofstadter in his book *Anti-Intellectualism in American Life* may have made too much of the role of religion. Churches did, after all, plant colleges wherever they went. True, these may have often been missionary training centers for representatives of heart religion. But they did open worlds of learning and became some of the better

academies in America. Yet he was correct in that Americans' frequent expressions of mistrust concerning intellect came from their attitude toward religion.

Was it self-consciousness? Did people simply not want to have their ignorance show? Was it laziness? Did they simply not want to sit down and think about the world of great change? Was there a false division of labor? Did they honestly think that after many centuries they could stop thinking and could begin only to act and to experience? Was it pride? After all, someone's experience cannot be tested, for it lies within in hidden recesses; but one's intellectual achievements can be assessed just as the buildings and works of his hands can be appraised. Maybe some simply feared they would not measure up. Was there a misreading of the Bible? Did the references to the fact that God chose "not many wise" lead some to misread what kind of wisdom was meant; in their eagerness to be among the elect, did they become mere fools instead of fools for Christ, childish instead of childlike? These have to be left in the form of suggestive and provocative questions. There are simply too many people and too many occasions to permit any satisfactory single answer or theory.

Whatever the causes, the fruits are evident. In American universities from the 1870s to the 1950s, during the whole period when these schools were developing, churches abdicated responsibility and religious learning was downgraded or segregated. A dozen universities allowed for a graduate school of divinity on the campus, but the churches knew even less what

to do with them than did the academy itself. In contemporary America one might almost note that seminaries devoted to heart religion are well-supported, while those that deal with theology suffer.

The institutes that bring religious people together find themselves regularly devoted to experience. Theology is not a prime topic at most. They become preoccupied with the human potential movement, bodily awareness, celebration, spiritual experiences—all of them legitimate but not by themselves the whole show of Christian life. Sermons are used for inspiring without informing, and are often an embarrassment to thoughtful people—most of whom eventually stay away. Religious thought outside the confines of denominations is overlooked. In religious publishing, people pay for every kind of book about how one experienced Jesus or the Holy Spirit, but first-rate books about how one might think about them go neglected.

All this despising of theology and intellect has a history. While it would be a bit crude to focus too much on one moment, the philosopher Alfred North Whitehead in *Adventures of Ideas* performed a service by taking one movement as a symbol of the American-style modern trend. He spoke of the Methodist or pietist movement, the eighteenth century recovery of heart religion as being a decisive example. After the Protestant Reformation and the Catholic counter-Reformation there had been a century of overrigid formulation of dogmatic systems. Then followed eighteenth century rationalism. Neither of these had much

to commend themselves to people who simply hungered for God.

Pietism and Methodism were democratic movements in which millions of European and later American Christians could take a vital part. In them a "direct intuitive appeal" was made to the minds of modern people. Hearts were strangely warmed. But, noted Whitehead, all around them a new world was being formed. Whereas early Christian fathers, medieval leaders, Reformation figures had all "argued" and constructed patterns of thought by which to address the new situations, in the new era people stopped arguing. It was a fateful moment, he thought, when the clergy of the Western world stopped appealing to constructive reason to set forth the place of their faith and experience.

Not all pietists or Methodists were mindless or formally intellectual. But in second and third generations of their movements thoughtless or militant people were ready to rule out what their founders merely neglected. And the modern world grew up progressively independent of religious norms. Where there was formulation, not all went well. Some nineteenth century Germans tried heroically to bring the world of faith and its larger environment together and often came up with embarrassing and even hair-raising heresies. But the failures elsewhere hardly served as justifications for the absence of attempts in America. Peter Berger once said that when modern Christians criticize the secular world for being secular, this is like blond parents criticizing their daughter for being blond. Thus in matters

theological, when believers criticize the world of thought for being godless, they are ill-poised to complain since they departed from the scene at which things godly could be empathically introduced.

American believers have often made up for the absence of fresh formulation by treasuring old books of theology. The idea is not all bad; "we are our fathers' shadows cast at noon," and not many contemporary people bring the genius or spirituality to their work that, say, Aquinas or Calvin brought to theirs. But new problems have emerged, and Christians who do not address them either become "keepers of the city of the dead," by dealing only with outworn formulae, or they idolize the old forms. Whitehead also had pointed out that while northwest European people were fighting a family war in the form of the Protestant Reformation and Catholic counter-Reformation, a new world of science and secular thought was being born and neither side addressed it.

In New England there had been a theological vision, but the churches compromised it to death or let it get stale. When a major theological mind took their experience and transmuted it into majestic thought, as Jonathan Edwards did, they misunderstood him and even banished him. In most of the colonies almost no theology worthy of later mention ever even emerged.

At the time of the birth of the nation two centuries ago the enlightened founding fathers sometimes talked in comprehensive philosophical terms about interpreting the religious world. But their practices spoke louder. They became cataloguers and counters of ob-

jects from the natural world: waterfalls and water-bugs, locusts and gemstones, and the like. They became preoccupied with how things work and making things work; with helping things travel harder or bang louder. They turned attention to laboratory and legislature. The timeless questions of human existence and meaning were often bracketed and shelved.

In the nineteenth century these preoccupations only developed. Christians often lived in two worlds. On one hand they kept on experiencing the spiritual realm, but they built a wall between it and the rest of their life. The line between sacred experience and secular thought grew. People became proud of their ignorance, establishing it as a sign of special faith. Europe was viewed negatively, for living in the past and for being complex. Theology was tied in with Europe as being part of the enemy's world.

In the parts of the church where old formulae were at least welcome, as at Princeton Seminary, a noted divine could brag that not an original idea had been born or uttered during his tenure at that school. Catholic immigrants imported catechisms and code books but seldom tried their hand at preparing fresh intellectual witness to life in America. And the evangelicals in the rough and tumble of the frontier were content at camp meeting and on the sawdust trail to let emotion and sensation take over as they berated the "infidels" with their human philosophy.

So at the end of the nineteenth century and well into the twentieth, American Catholics had not produced a single thinker who had to be reckoned with by Catho-

lics elsewhere. The American evangelicals divided their lives in two and made less and less of theology and human learning. Jews were a partial exception; their renewal movements did involve basic attempts at formulations of religious thought for the American environment. But the achievements were also generally meager.

The problem with neglect is that it gives a one-sided view of what religion is about and it circumscribes the sphere of religion. In effect it asks thoughtful people to leave their thought behind them when they enter the sanctuary. And it denies the religious vision of most faiths, because it abandons the world to its own devices and allows for it to construct worlds of thought unchallenged or uninformed by people who are off somewhere enjoying private spiritual experiences at the expense of a larger truth.

-11-

Religion without Demands

RELIGIOUS AMERICA, at the time of its bicentennial, is viewed in the eyes of the world as a self-seeking society. While there have been instances of generosity on the part of American citizens, these have usually been expressions of a policy that was designed to benefit the government, the churches, or economic interests. And individual efforts have been so relatively meager, marked by such little skimming off the top of American wealth, that the nation is often resented even by those who are supposed to be beneficiaries of the policies.

"By their fruits you shall know them." That is a biblical reminder of the fact that religion is to be judged by its products. Since America's religious organizations devote themselves very much to such ethical language, they have a need to be judged by the measure they themselves employ. The person or people who receive the benefits of another's right action are supposed to be viewed as of intrinsic value. The person

who serves or helps them is not to do it to enhance the image of himself, his church, his corporation, or his nation. The Good Samaritan did not do good because it would be of use in public relations; the story is told accidentally, as if its main subject would have little care whether or not it would be told. He did what the situation demanded. He did not take his captive audience ("strapped to his ass") and preach a sermon, hand out tracts, or advertise Samaritan virtues. He gave of himself, his goods, his risks, as ends in themselves.

Christians, of course, have always had trouble with such actions. They share mortality and selfishness. They have always had difficulties knowing how to serve Christ in his neighbors and brothers. Those believers who prospered have often closed their eyes to poverty outside their house and gates. History is full of examples of comfortable religious people soothing their conscience by giving meager alms, advertising the pittances of their charities. Fortunately for them, modernity has brought with it a rising sense of conscience so that people without explicit religious faith have teamed up with believers who are exceptionally thoughtful. Some governmental policies and those of other nonreligious voluntary associations pick up ancient ideas of Christian charity and make them workable in the modern world. The churches have taken active roles. But there is no danger that anyone will be led by their actions to think that humanitarian causes receive high priority, as a survey of the scene quickly suggests.

A look at the budget always helps. Where one's

treasure is, there is his heart also; a budget or a list of expenditures often tells more about values and priorities than would any number of official pronouncements. Has American religion produced open hearts and eyes? A familiar kind of assessment was made some years ago by sociologist Gerhard Lenski. He posed an issue: suppose India were in famine. The United States had enough wheat to help face the situation; there was a local oversupply. The boats were available. There was only one question: it could not be guaranteed in advance that sending the grain to India would not have some consequences for the American economy. Should this nation take the risks?

In general the findings suggested that the nonreligious liberal political community would be most ready to take the risk. After it, the Jewish groups would be most ready to share, no matter what happened in America. Moving further through the concentric circles, Roman Catholics who were not active in their churches did worse than Jews but better than practicing Catholics. Finally, nonpracticing Protestants did better than Protestants. It was the active, disciplined, church-going Protestants who were most concerned that risks would have to be eliminated first. They would have to know most about whether the economy would in any way be jeopardized. If they had these assurances, then they could help feed the hungry. It goes without saying that such an approach is not compatible with the biblical mandates for God's children.

That instance deals only with attitudes and with a situation that did not occur. In actual life, the budgets

again show how aware America's believers are of human need and their call to face it. Few dollars gathered through religious organizations leave the home churches; fewer are used for foreign work; fewest reach people in physical need overseas. Where missions survive, these tend to be of the "faith mission" variety. By this we mean that independent fundamentalists who believe very clear teachings about what they want to accomplish in the souls of others are most successful at raising funds and motivating missionaries. Rarely do they talk about physical needs at all; their chief concerns have to do with the souls of non-Americans. They are not to be faulted for their diagnosis. People do not live by bread alone. What is more, many of these missionaries do bring bread along with the word they teach. It would be foolish to criticize those who keep some sort of awareness of and love for the world's poor in mind, and let everyone else who has no vision at all off easily. But the faith missions do proportionately little by way of humanitarian work.

Wherever the main line churches have redesigned their missions so that they could stress the role of "fraternal workers" or pour their main energies into the building of clinics, hospitals, work camps, or schools, they have suffered lack of support. People do not sustain their imaginations for such projects. The World Council of Churches and other international agencies have experienced drastic cutbacks in support funds. Many of them have despaired of the idea of winning their clienteles over to seeing the developing nations' needs on their own terms.

In one instance where American religious groups have been active overseas, American Jews in their support of Israel, one need hardly go so far as to take away from great humanitarian achievements if he also notes a mixture of motives. Many Jews themselves will admit that they need Israel as a means of securing Jewish identity; that subject is almost as important as finding a homeland for new refugees. Or the support of Israel is sometimes based on expressions of guilt by wealthy Americans who do not want to be part of the immigration to Israel. Even in this best case, then, the world sees American believers as involved with extending NATO, Western technology, and markets into the Middle East as in looking at the needs of all the people on that scene.

Those overseas illustrations can be extended into the domestic sphere by a glance at the budgets and activities of religious organizations on the home front. Each year during the 1960s the American groups spent $1000 million (translated: $1 billion) adding to their physical plants. This made architects and builders happy, and often supplied needed facilities. But the outlays were often for plush, competitive, overlapping programs that served to insulate practitioners of religion from a vision of how other people lived. Whoever disbelieves this need only to pick up the budget of almost any local church in America to see how little is spent on anything beyond its own four walls. The indictment is telling, because most of the rhetorical appeals suggest that the proportion is reversed; most of the self-advertisements of religious organizations deal with

what they are doing in support of a needy world. The churches were to have been the main custodians of the charitable impulse; if they fail so miserably to see their neighbor's needs, who will lead?

Here we have spoken of religious groups serving outsiders. At the same time, they also organize themselves in such ways that even the needs of fellow-believers are rarely met. Thus in any metropolitan area, even churches of the same denomination that share one creed and style of worship rarely put themselves together in any way that might make their resources available to those in need. The exurbanites do not look at suburban need; the suburbanites overlook urbanites; urbanites turn away from the ghetto. Rather than organize "spokes" from the center of the city to the wealthiest areas and make people interdependent, the poor churches have to suffer attrition and death while the wealthy ones live to themselves. They build houses of God whose most expensive and extensive floor space is used one or two hours a week, while not many miles away people have no place for shelter or care.

The American churches, despite their injunctions, have permitted people individually also to lapse into self-seeking. The business creed of the churches and synagogues serves to assure everyone that they are free to use religious symbols to justify their competitive economic ways of life—so long as they are then personally generous. But the secular world has long since learned that per capita charities of church people, for causes beyond the needs of the churches themselves, by no means outstrip what nonbelievers give and do.

In some respects—moving now from budgetary questions to programs—the patterns of church life can even make it less attractive to people to be of service to anyone but themselves. Very often the quality of one's faith is measured by the number of evenings per week that members are on the church premises. Their goodness is marked by the way in which they express loyalty to their own kind. They become self-protective, full of illusions, unable to comprehend the ways of life of different people. Meanwhile the churches provide them with prayers, liturgies, and worship forms that suggest to them that they are giving alms and thus carrying on God's works in the world.

American religion as a justification for self-seeking has a long history. No one should take anything away from those believers who pioneered in humanitarian work. But their ideology was also used to justify personal gain and the development of prejudice against others. "Godliness is in league with riches," said a prominent Episcopal bishop in the nineteenth century.

The roots of the problem lie much deeper. What is remembered from colonial times? Who can recall that Christian colonists persevered in their works of love toward American Indians? Are the efforts by believers to relieve the bad circumstances of black slaves anything more than very rare exceptions? What *is* remembered is the story of amazing and ever-increasing successes by the already successful. Religion came to be used as a way to justify the taking of personal gain. If the Puritans came with a sense of just prices or fair economic life, they quickly abandoned this and encour-

aged laissez faire attitudes. They bred a spirit of aggressive earning and piling up; in such circumstances, the follow-through about giving for or serving people of different ways was perfunctory and forgotten.

In the nineteenth century some change came with the spread of a "benevolent empire," but its limits were also apparent. During these years the philosophy of the "busy bee," the frantically active American developed. In this period charity was professionalized. A person could pay someone else to do the works of love. Complex organizations made this possible. A man could spend his week as an industrialist who by caprice or to suit his purpose could put 30,000 people out of work on a Friday and then on Sunday could write out a check that would support a church in the slums.

Critics of the humanitarian enterprise of nineteenth century American religious people have no difficulty pointing to its limits. More energy went into denouncing the vices of individual prostitutes, drunks, or profane persons than into changing the circumstances that made their way of life plausible or necessary. More went into reform of manners or the spread of religious ideas than into reform of society or the spread of justice. When religious groups did organize to help the poor, they often did so on terms that were demeaning: first you listen to my sermon, and then I'll give you a lunch. The agencies that got this close to the poor—one thinks of the Salvation Army—should not be chastised when one compares them to those that remained at a distance. Here the point is only made that

their mode of charity was also often condescending. And many churchly activities actually served to reinforce bad policies. Religious people would help bind up the wounds left by a vicious social order; they did not consider it in place or beneficial for them to risk anything to help change that order.

Those who joined in the "errand of mercy" in the nineteenth century left behind diaries that showed them often to be expressing their own egos. I do not mean that they were hypocritical or full of knavery; instead, they simply built around themselves and their supporters an ethos that let them give some hours or dollars for people in bad circumstances without in any way calling into question the way of life that produced the evils.

In the late nineteenth century conditions worsened. In the earlier years the head of a retail store might attend evangelistic rallies and sing the hymns; he would inconvenience himself. His grandson more likely only remembered the faith. He tried to overcome the unethical aspects of his life and soothe his conscience while starting a seminary or a university somewhere or other. Most of the "robber barons" did. There is no point in focusing long or exclusively on them. They were a tiny minority. They did, however, become the ideal in thousands of sermons and textbooks. Rising young people were to aspire to copy them. Great memorial churches were erected in their name, their façades towering over broad avenues that were themselves only yards from horrendous slums.

In recent times there has been much criticism of the

kinds of ethics that permitted so much institutional self-seeking and personal self-aggrandizement while the world burned. Yet the criticism has not served effectively to cause people to turn around. Secular humanists regularly point to the disproportionate energies religious institutions give to the survival, good name, and good conditions of their institutions. They neglect the good ends for which the institutions purportedly exist.

"Let's join the human race," was the call of a pamphlet title by Stringfellow Barr a couple of decades ago. He showed the gap between religious America and a sea of need. A gadget-filled paradise remained suspended in a hell of international insecurity, according to Reinhold Niebuhr. The churches and other religious organizations as often as not added to the illusions about that paradise.

- 12 -

Worship of the Status Quo

IF PROPHETIC religion is designed to "afflict the comfortable," another side of religion comforts the afflicted. Few analysts of religion would criticize the attempt to have it apply to all of life and to make it possible for people to find comfort. However there is always the danger that comforting religion be used to sanctify the present, to endorse the status quo.

In the terms of biblical religion, attempts to announce "Peace! Peace! when there is no peace" is a denial of prophetic responsibility. Efforts to tie in God's purposes with the world as it is are identified as idolatry. Prophetic faith is to be connected with the future purposes of God, with the justice, righteousness, and love that he alone can bring. Yet people are always tempted to take refuge from and find security in the world they have put together—especially if they can find some way to link it with the purposes of God by some translation or other. Whenever the present is

overaffirmed, the needs of others in an imperfect world tend to be overlooked; people apply arbitrary and false standards to their own doings; they confuse their images with the divine reality.

Self-congratulatory religion is dangerous to the self, for the person taken up with it loses perspective and empathy. It is most dangerous in the church or other religious organization, where the temptations of pride grow. The believer takes too much credit for his part in the bond between the divine or sacred himself and forgets that, as Abraham Lincoln put it, "The Almighty has his own purposes." The reason why this is dangerous is because the church is supposed to be a special custodian of the divine law, a treasure house in which sacred symbols are to be kept fresh and creative. When people take these captive and confuse their purposes with God's it is hard for the law to be heard and the creative symbols to find expression in the world.

Even more dangerous are the attempts to identify God's purposes with a nation's way of life. Sometimes these attempts focus on what is called "civil religion," a possibly creative way of seeing the nation itself as a matrix or repository of religious symbols and purpose. But the "way of life" religion may encompass more. It can include behavior patterns, customs, mores, and sanctions for success seeking. At bicentennial time Americans look out on a powerful and confused nation. They know that if they are too negative about it in its time of troubles it may not recover. But they also see a precedent for recognizing that self-satisfaction has been equally dangerous.

Charles Henderson wrote an exposition of *The Nixon Theology* in which he showed how former President Richard M. Nixon and evangelist Billy Graham tended to use the same symbols. However when Graham spoke of "the promise of God," Nixon spoke of the promise of the nation itself or of its children. When Graham spoke of the nation as being "under God," Nixon tended to speak of the nation "as God," as itself the object of devotion and reverence. There is no reason to single out Richard M. Nixon as a special confuser of this issue; the temptation has been present among many of his predecessors who came to recognize the White House as a jolly good pulpit—which is how Theodore Roosevelt thought of it. Nor need one be a president to ascribe to the nation, race, tribe, church, or club the attributes one should reserve for God.

If the temptations to lose the prophetic note are timeless in religion, it is legitimate to ask why anyone should worry about the form this takes in America. A special circumstance arose in this "first new nation," the place where religious voluntaryism on a large scale was born. I refer to what has been called "the politics of pulpit and pew." In that relation, the congregations are in effect customers or clients of ministers and other leaders. If he presses them too hard they will go elsewhere. There are no captive audiences where persuasion, not coercion has its domain. Ask any honest southern preacher why he does not unload the whole burden of what is on his heart in light of the Word of God. He will answer that it will be his last sermon; the

people will simply drift off to a church that has "sold out" more than his own. If the members are customers, they are also bosses. They can, in most churches, do the hiring and firing. While congregations have shown notable tolerance for every kind of foible and folly, not all of them will allow themselves to be "pushed" inordinately by a preacher who questions too many of the assumptions by which the group lives.

The foreign visitors to the United States in the nineteenth century regularly remarked about the politics of pulpit and pew and what this did to prophetic proclamation. Few of them complained that there was too little "hell-fire and damnation." From some points of view the spokesmen for God spoke vehemently enough to suffice. But they focused on individual vices and other issues that either titillated the audiences or left them routes of escape. Let the proclaimer of the word apply it to the truly troubling matters—slavery was a good instance at the time many of them wrote—and his career would end. Alexis de Toqueville and others spoke of a safe circle within which a minister had freedom and beyond which he dared not go. That circle is still drawn.

On every scale there remains a temptation, inevitable in religion but intensified in America, to have people use divine symbols to enhance the human status quo. Thus in one-to-one relations people do not find it difficult to engage in tongue-lashings about petty elements in personality or ways of life. But they tend to connive to prevent facing up to basic faults. In middle-class America, few are free to question assumptions

about the social order. Whoever wonders about basic change need take only one look at the typical Christian congregation: it will almost automatically be for "law and order" at the expense of the risks of freedom. Its members will almost always demand a different system of justice and retribution for ghetto delinquents than it will for suburban vandals, the "nice kids" who are on Saturday night pranks—and whose parents can pay for the damage and keep the event out of the newspapers.

Local congregations seem to draw much of their strength from their contribution to the status quo. It is true that all lives need some balance, stability, and status quo; but there is a temptation for Christian cells to overdo their contribution by showing how God would have them keep things as they are. Several years ago someone hung out a banner: "The Seven Last Words of the Church: We Never Did It That Way Before." Everyone smiles knowingly; seldom are there exceptions to local churches' social conservatism and love of the routinely sanctioned. In more dramatic terms: suppose "the Devil" had a day off and was free to go to and fro in the earth. He visits a particular community and wants to create problems for that institution or group of people that does most to promote justice and good. Would he waste time with most local churches? Are they not harmless? Are they not out of his way, on by-paths?

Do church people live up to their possibilities as agents of change for good? We must assume that all of them can be brought to see that there is a gap be-

tween the good society pictured by the prophets and the real society in which we live. Whoever does not see that cannot recognize hunger, poverty, malaise, and despair. Believers are in the world not only to enjoy the blessings of God but to share in his loving works toward people. Change involves risk and innovation. Has a poll-taker or interviewer ever come across a congregation (excepting, perhaps, maverick experimental communities built around a specific prophetic intention) whose people are ahead of their neighbors in thinking toward or working toward change? They usually show up as the most safe and cautious element in the neighborhood. They seek leaders who reinforce their world as it has been put together and will not let them evoke biblical or other religious symbols that would challenge it.

In the public sphere the absence of those who will protest society's basic courses is also evident. "Nowadays we do not stone the prophets; we invite them to dinner." We make best sellers of their first searching books and thus begin the process of buying them off. We have them golf with the mayor or preach in the East Room of the White House. If someone comes along who can stir the conscience we find his or her flaws and give them the widest possible media exposure on the assumption that this will compromise such persons. It usually does. (Whether any of the saints in the calendar or biblical heroes would have survived FBI surveillance and CBS coverage is questionable.)

The purpose in this little accounting is not to suggest that somewhere there is a place where pure and

unspotted prophets exist above the realm of taint and compromise. In one sense no human has credentials to judge others. But there are special dangers in a free society where religious voices are uncommonly dependent upon clienteles and customers, as it were, for them to be silenced. What is more, most of us recognize so much good in the American resolutions that we are doubly suspicious about any attempts to change them. Paul Tillich once remarked that no American group is more idolatrous of the status quo than the one that has "revolution" built into its name: Daughters of the American Revolution. They would not recognize that for which they purportedly stand in loving memory if it came marching down their street. Our industrial revolution was generally as successful as our political one was. The British sociologist of religion, David Martin, argues that if one says "Texas Baptist millionaire" he receives knowing winks of recognition. To the world this phrase conjures up the image of someone who wants an "otherworldly" Gospel full of Christ's references to a drastically different kingdom. But he is also known as a very secular or worldly man, nervous about any Christian proclamation that might call into question existing relations in the economic order—unless it calls for a repeal of recent changes and moves back toward an earlier form of less regulated economy.

Needless to say, lest I lose a hearing and sound prophetic: not all Texas Baptist millionaires have to fill Martin's stereotype. Nor do you have to be Texan, Baptist, or a millionaire to idolize the economic and

social patterns of the America that was or is. There are predispositions, however, among the religiously well-situated and comfortable to do most to resist change even if change promises justice and health for new groups of fellow citizens. Nowhere does this religious identification with one pattern of life show up so enthusiastically as in the civil realm. The national flag in the sanctuary is a more sacred, less-to-be-tampered with object than is a church flag, a cross, or a Star of David. Nothing calls forth more emotion on the floor of a denominational convention than a suggestion that not everything in national society is just and liberating.

Such attitudes have a history. While America has known men and women of prophetic character, ordinarily its leaders are expected to be safe. The Anglican clerics of Virginia in pre-Revolutionary days conceived of themselves as gentlemen-chaplains to the establishment. In New England they more frequently were chaplains to the community; but if they sometimes sounded "revolutionary" over against England, they were almost wholly captive of the interests of their congregations, as Alan Heimert has shown in respect even to the liberal clergy of colonial Boston, in his book *Religion and the American Mind*. Heimert showed that one stood the best chance of being upsetting and prophetic if he were an itinerant backwoods revivalist, and not a fashionable preacher of revolution against England and for the American status quo in the towns.

The American Revolution brought what almost all

of us would regard as the kind of society in which we want to live and one in which it is possible to live a largely free religious life. But it must be remembered that the founding fathers were not particularly interested in building in a principle by which that society might be open to revision when there are basic flaws. Not that one would expect constitutionalists to do so; it is their task to build in stability. They did well, through their checks-and-balance system. But this governmental solution should not be confused, as it often is, with the kingdom of God. The status quo that resulted from the birth of the republic did not assure freedom to the free. And whole races were excluded from its charters of liberty.

During the century when legal provision for such freedom was being fought for, those who argued the case on biblical grounds were regularly dismissed and despised, harassed and physically assaulted. During the century after emancipation those who worked for justice for the freed often suffered the same fate. Similarly, in the industrial realm, few were those who worked to let the liberating message of religion reach those who had no voice in labor-management affairs. Most of the hard-fought and even harder-won gains that are now taken for granted had to be secured by people who had to move outside and even oppose the main line religious forces. Most of these thought that to permit labor to organize, for example, was contrary to the laws of nature and a divine plan. Need we add that not all organization of labor produces divine styles of justice, nor that the Bible or similar religious docu-

ments charter a particular form of organizing life? American labor, after *its* revolution, can be as resistant to change as the Daughters of the American Revolution have been about their revolution and any innovations.

That status quo has been sanctioned by celebrity preachers, by middle class Christian voters, by those who call down the name of God on any American cannon, no matter at whom they are pointed or under what circumstances and for what purposes. Instead the citizens seek out the leaders who assure them that God wants them to be rich and successful, to create themselves and then worship their creator. If a prophet comes along: invite him to dinner and buy him out. Stoning is too messy.

Epilogue: Turning Con to Pro

Too MUCH criticism can be destructive. For one thing, the prophet or critic can soon confuse himself or herself with God speaking. It is not difficult to find some biblical passages or resource from one religious tradition or another and then link it up with one's own conceptions of how society should be or act. From that point, it is also easy to keep hearing the sound of one's own voice or to share the judgments of one's own group and to stop hearing anything else. Someone has called this disease "propheticism." It can be an expression of an unbalanced personality, the result of a weak ego that constantly needs reinforcement. Or it can result from simply a bad reading of a situation. After all, in the course of two centuries it is possible, is it not, to find traces of God acting positively in society. Have not religious people now and then responded faithfully?

Paul Tillich once divided the Christian message into

what he called "Protestant principle" and "Catholic substance." With the two adjectives he did not mean to refer to two clusters of church bodies. Instead he was arguing that fulfilled religion has a protesting dimension. One cannot always and only be PRO in respect to the surrounding world. Divine judgment does not let us rest with that. Someone is always going to be left out in such observations. But just as quickly as the CON is asserted and the fault-finders take over, religious people often forget their privileges and responsibilities so far as making a deposit in the culture is concerning.

"Catholic substance" is the result. Tillich meant by this the caring for earth, community, and person. Out of it grows the impulse to build cathedrals, sing songs, engage in political action, provide institutions for the care of others. Along with it goes a pattern of interpretation that allows a person to appreciate the achievements. Those who only protest have little to lose when society disintegrates. They have invested almost nothing in it. But those who have left a deposit of Catholic substance have to care about what it is that they have shared in making. After two hundred years there are some questions that might lead the critics to answer with positive affirmations: Yes, good things have happened here. God has not left himself without witness.

A question or two can grow out of each of the topics or ways of looking that we have employed to see American life in broad outline.

A nation that drips and overflows with resources

could hardly help but have materialistic dimensions. The hills and plains, the mines and factories all conspire to present people with the things of the world. It is hard not to love them. But should it not also be noticed that in the midst of the cornucopian splendors, men and women have consistently also kept their attentions on spiritual matters? The spirituality may often have been superficial but, given the distractions, should not one also ask, "Compared to what?" How does the soul of America look when compared not only with saints of the past but with fellow citizens of the world today?

Obsessed and jumpy as Americans are about *now* and *tomorrow,* is it not remarkable that again and again they have chartered long looks at the past? Even their nostalgia and sense that their "good old days," though this may not be because of any informed historical inquiry, shows that people love what has gone before, pay attention to what their forefathers have loved, and want to pass on some elements of tradition to those who will follow.

Americans so often force each other to go it alone. Some of them even make an ideology out of doing so, and argue that competition between individuals is at the heart of American life and is the will of God. But this nation has not only been a jungle of competitors, a wilderness of lonely pioneers. Is it not also true that they have helped bear each other's burdens, have cared about each other's needs, have established patterns for coming together that lead some visitors to see us as a nation of belongers?

Love of place can lead to idolatry of tribe. We like our own darkness, can live with our own superstitions. While Americans have had some good reason to cherish their own local place, is it not noteworthy that few people have ever done as much as they have to travel, to communicate, to give and hear words, to try to gain some empathy with people who are far away?

The annals of religious prejudice are long and sad. Histories of intolerance, of people who were near each other's throats over dogma and practice, are plentiful. No one should be surprised at that, given the long shadow of holy wars in history. Is it not surprising, then, that hundreds of religious groups have learned to get along in a world where getting along religiously is not yet a commonplace? What shall we make of the many movements of tolerance and the countless signs of neighborliness that have come to characterize religious life here?

If religious prejudice is bad, racial styles are worse. Lives have been ruined and lost by it; the prejudiced against and the prejudicial ones both suffer. Those who inherited the burdens of slave-importation, those who suffered economic hardship as a result of the presence of other races were victims as well as agents of the racist system. But while few will brag about progress, is there not some word to be said about the moments of break-through, of religious realization of reconciliation?

Clerics have been frequently enough engaged in self-seeking quests for status accompanied by evasions of leadership responsibilities. They have then kept the

laity confused or suppressed. But should not a word be said for the marvellously frequent interactions between enterprising and supportive lay people and the men and women who in ministering to them were secure in expressions of their own personalities and yet could yield and share status?

Males should blush in embarrassment or cry in shame when they go over the records of American religion. They know that women were in religious majorities but hardly show up in the indices of the books. But is this not changing, and do not the new stories unfold a dramatic sequence of liberating events?

Yes, people can use religion to their own purposes. But what should be said of the society that has been busiest turning religion to the service of others?

One could have wished for far more intellectual enterprise in relation to the faith and experience. But despite meager resources and many preoccupations, people of genius or mere talent have taken second looks, have been reflective. Should not a good word be said for American theologizing, once its own patterns are understood?

American religion has been a buyer's market; there have been many options, so the sellers can go cheap with their wares and offer, offer, offer. Is it not also to be noticed that not everyone follows the peddlers of religion, that again and again people have turned serious about the claims religion makes on them?

Seldom has it been difficult for people to look around them and celebrate the society as it is. But is there not also another story, the one that sees men and women

moved by spiritual impulses trying to right the wrongs? Have there not also been prophets?

These questions imply the beginnings of answers. For those who cannot sustain too sour and dour a look at American flaws, there is another story. Its outlines are easily available. Simply flip this book over, and start from the other side.

149